Psalm of the Hyacinth
From the Orphic Bible

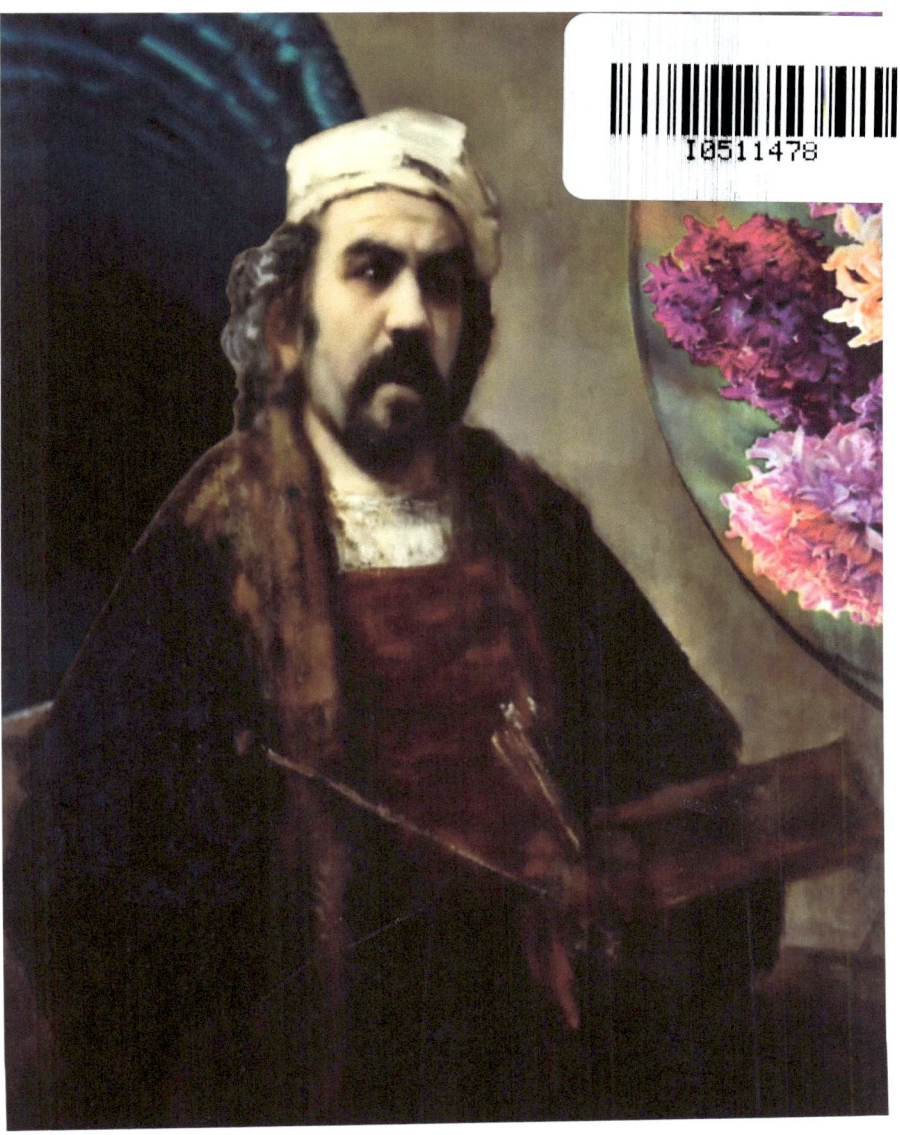

Kit Ludlow

Copyright © 2022 kit ludlow

All rights reserved.

ISBN: 9798847100359 (color)
ISBN: 9798847213714 (B&W)

IG: kitludlow

For Mo Chlann

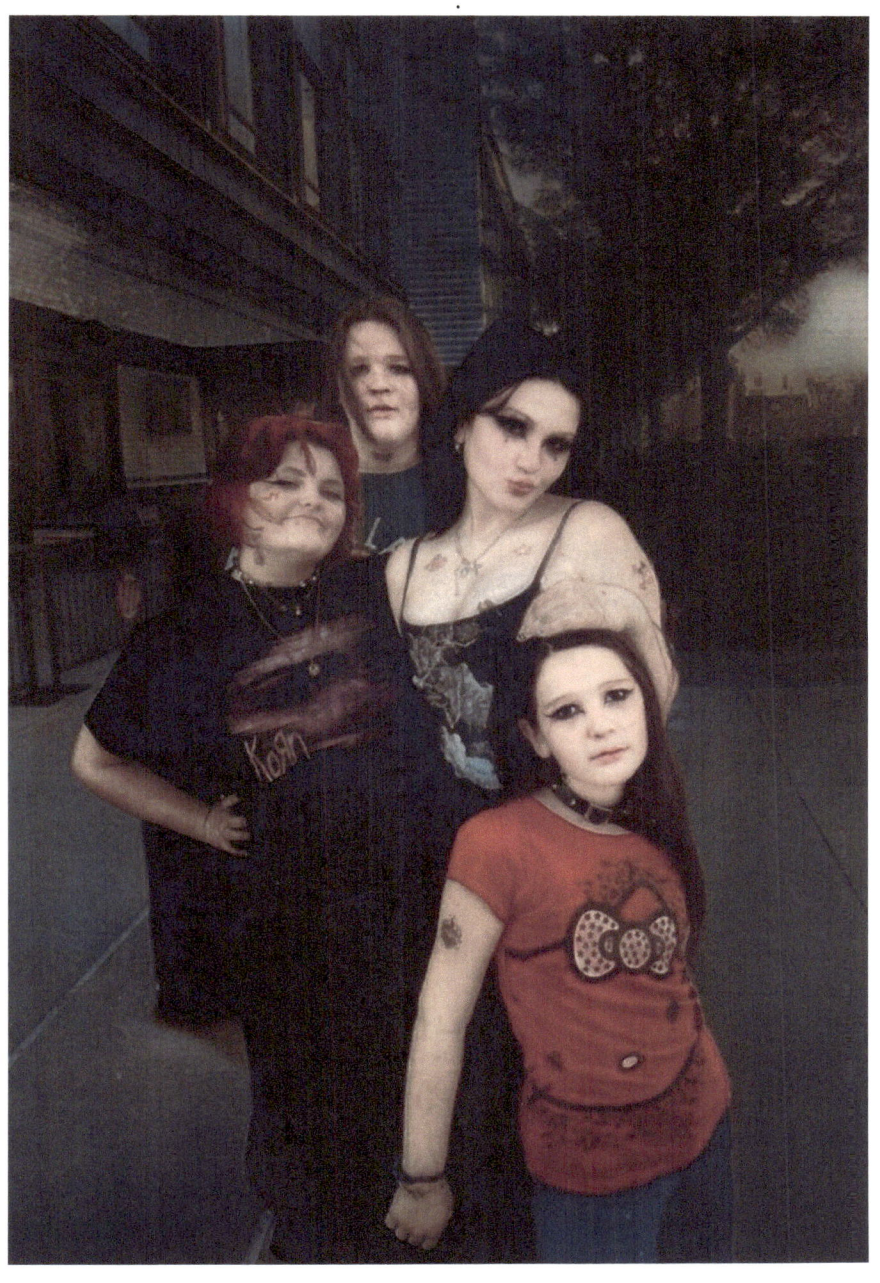

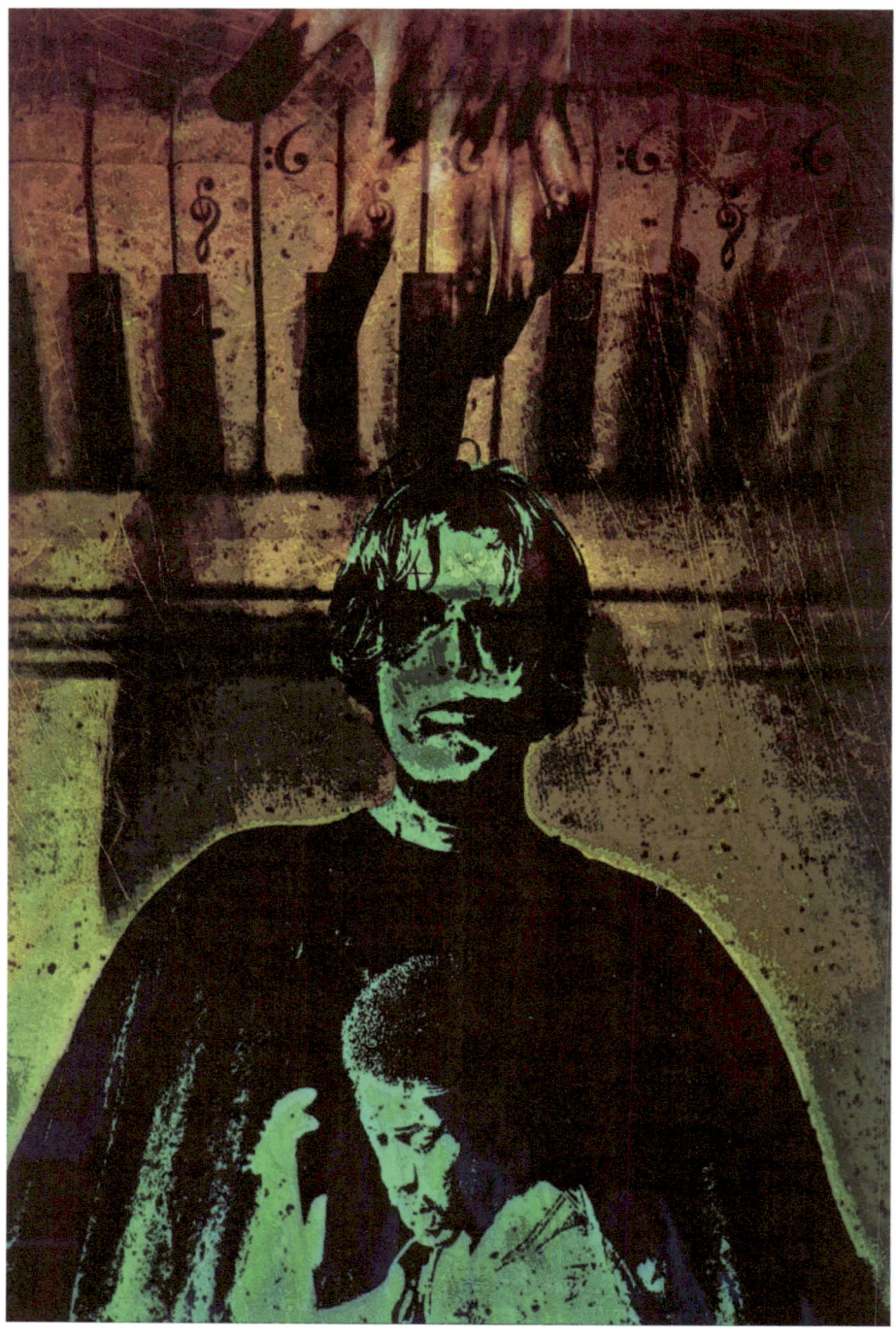

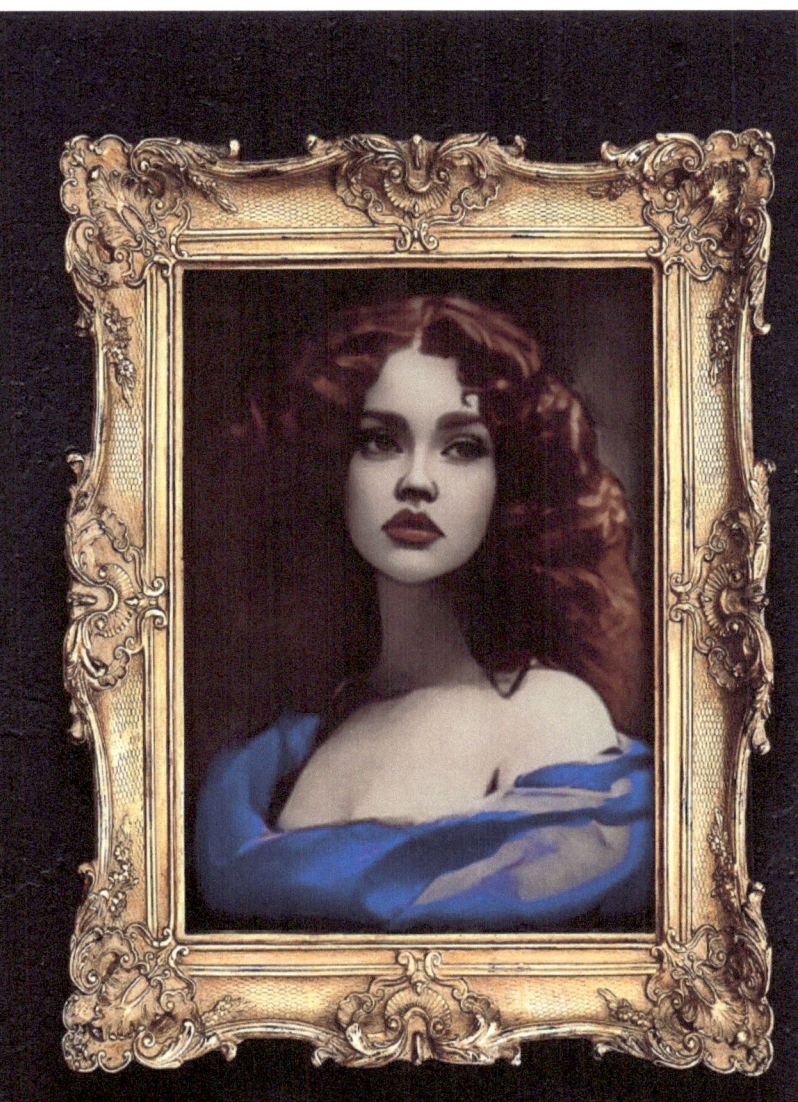

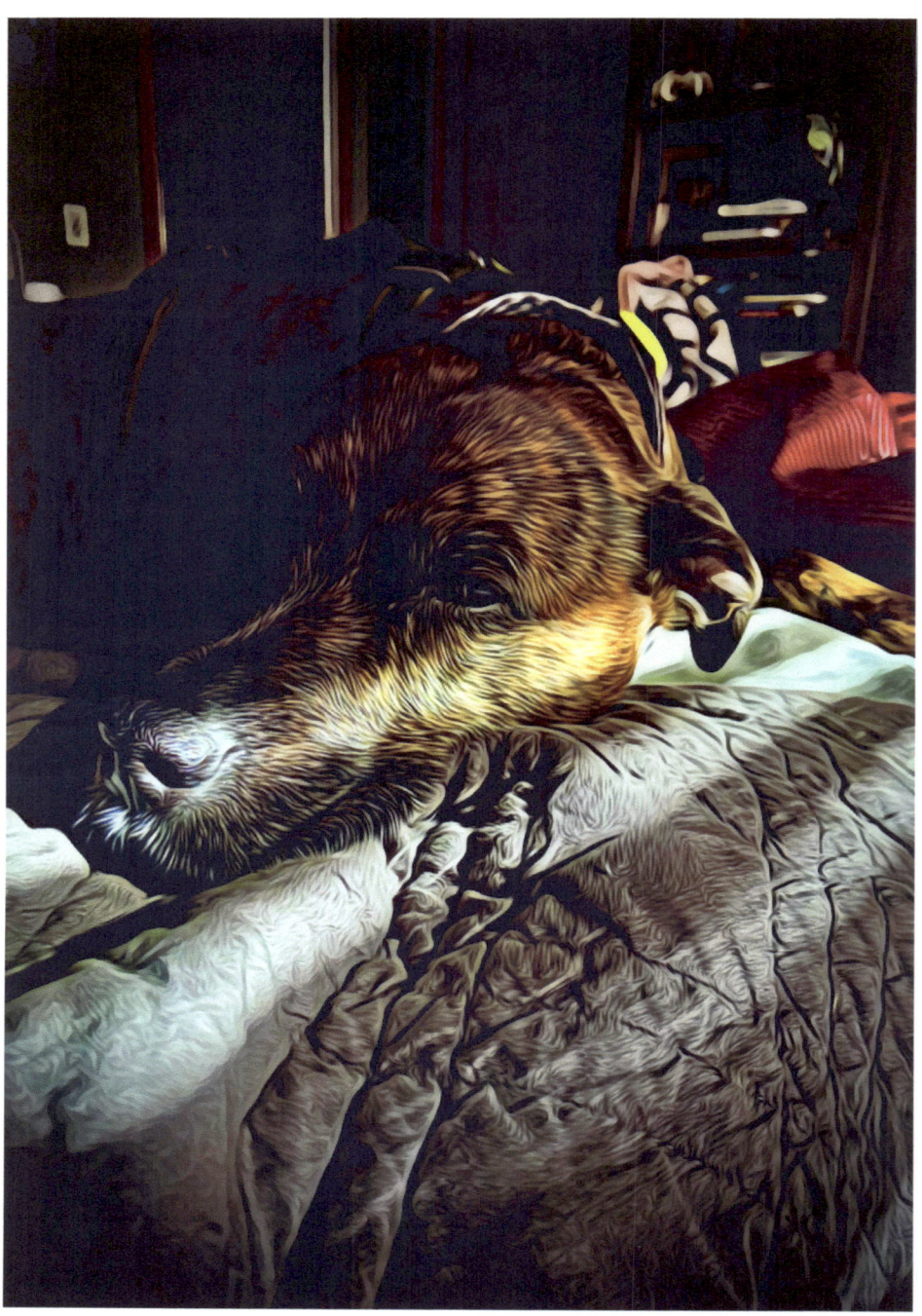

ON THE TEXT

"The Psalm of Hyacinth" is a three-sonnet poem written from the point-of-view of Orpheus. It is told after his failed attempt to retrieve Eurydice from Hades, his years of wandering and the dismemberment from the Maenads of Dionysus.

The poem is from the Orphic Bible, a collection of Orpheus' poems and writings. The poems have no elements of Orphism or any other mystery religion from the ancient world. Many of those works survive in references from the poets of antiquity. This poem is a supplemental work to Kit Ludlow's "Orpheus". "Book One: City of Time" is available now. "Book Two: Lotus of the Outis" will be release near the fall of 2022.

For updates, artwork and progress on "Orpheus", follow Kit Ludlow on Instagram (unique ID: kitludlow). You can also view artwork of other upcoming books.

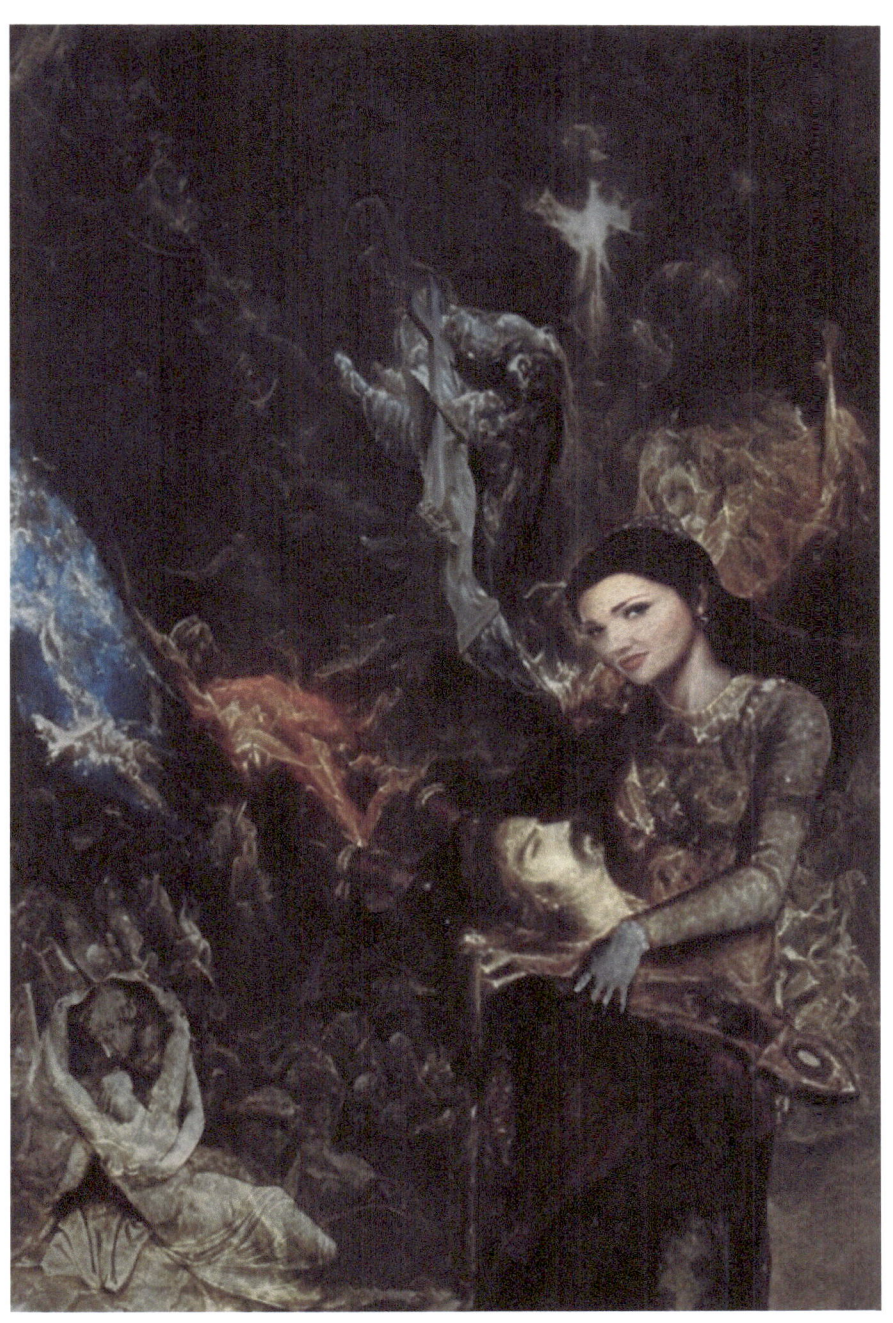

Torn apart and barely breathing.

Psalm of the Hyacinth

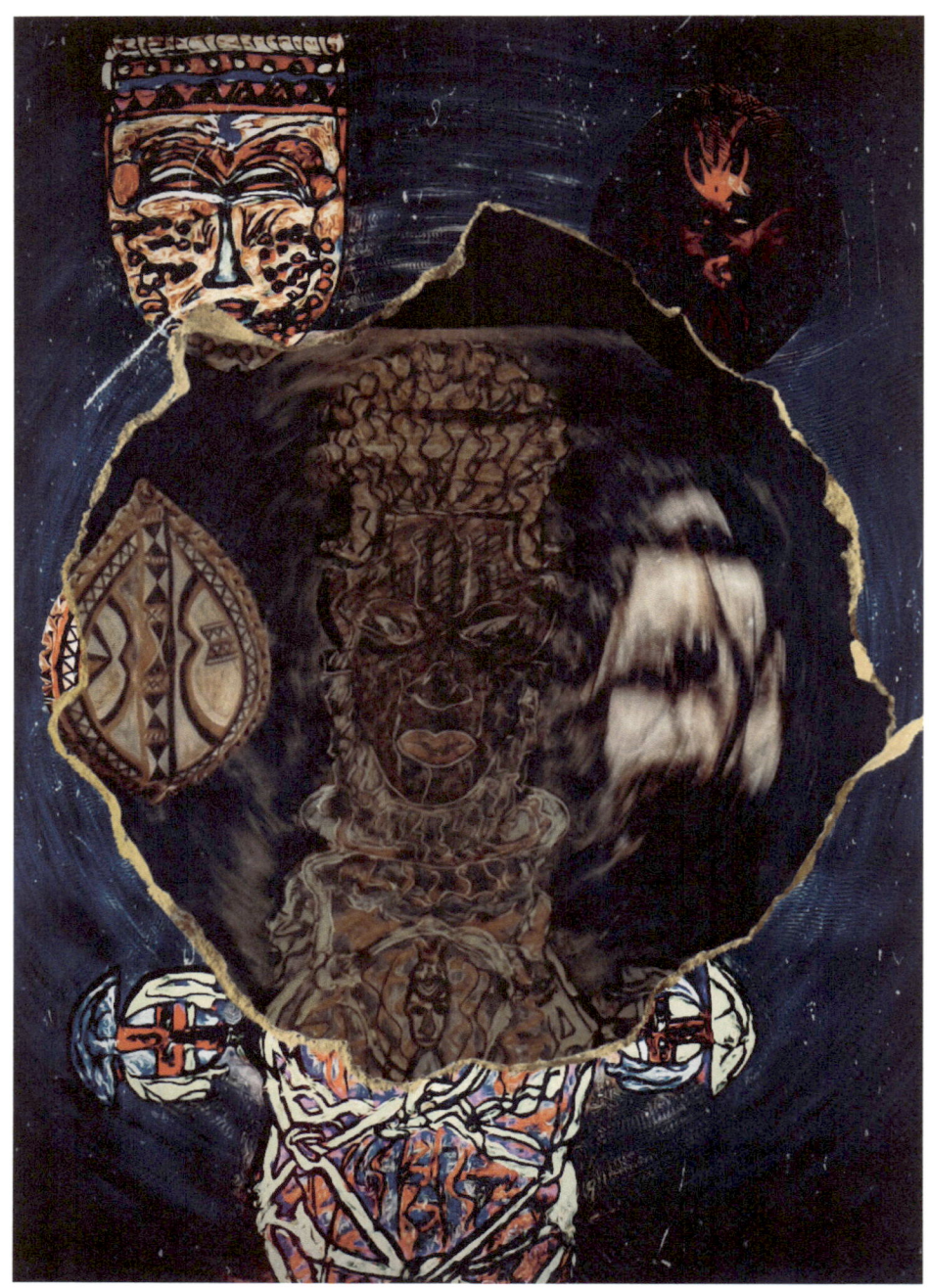

Left on the shore.

Psalm of the Hyacinth

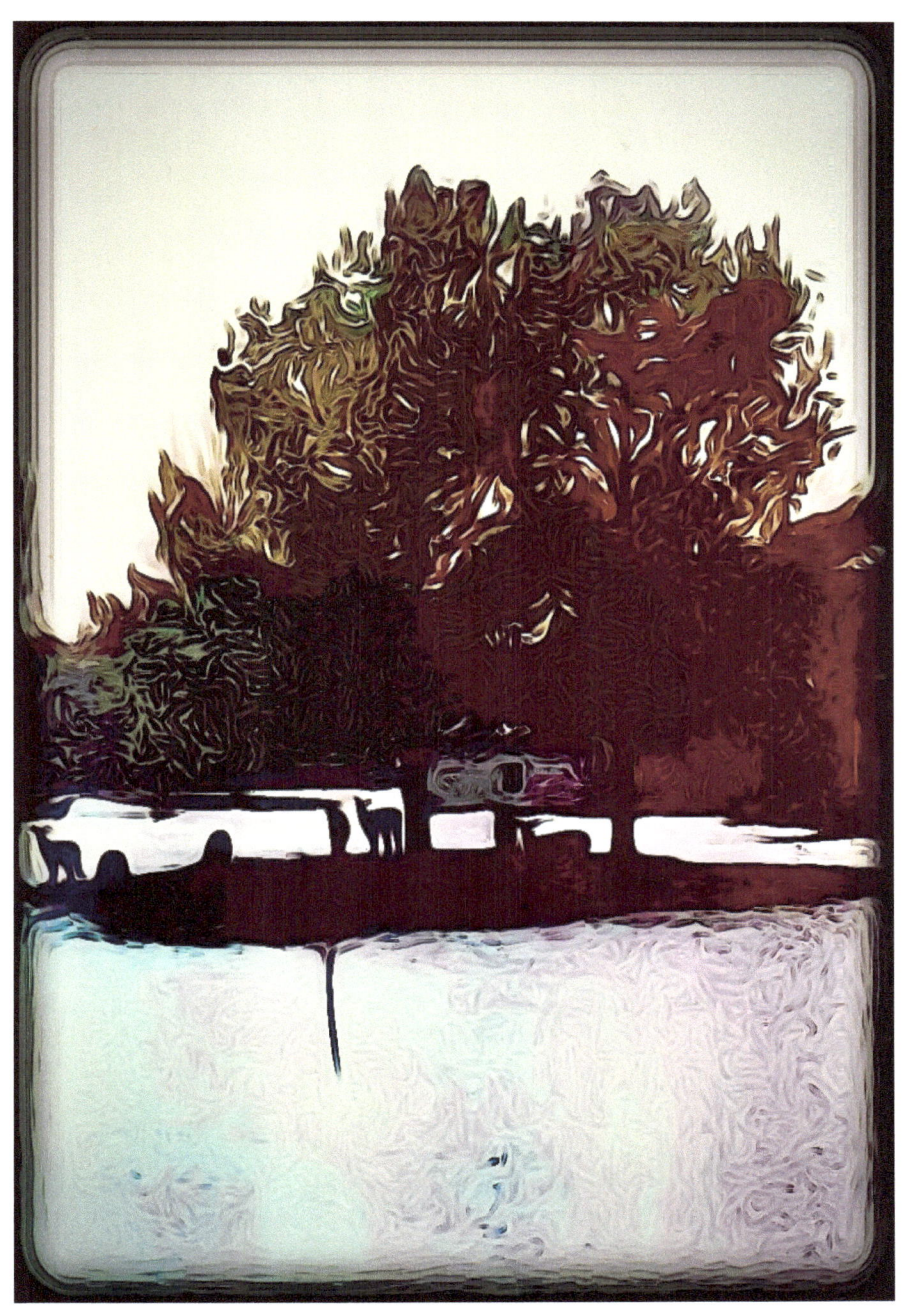

Silence plenty.

Psalm of the Hyacinth

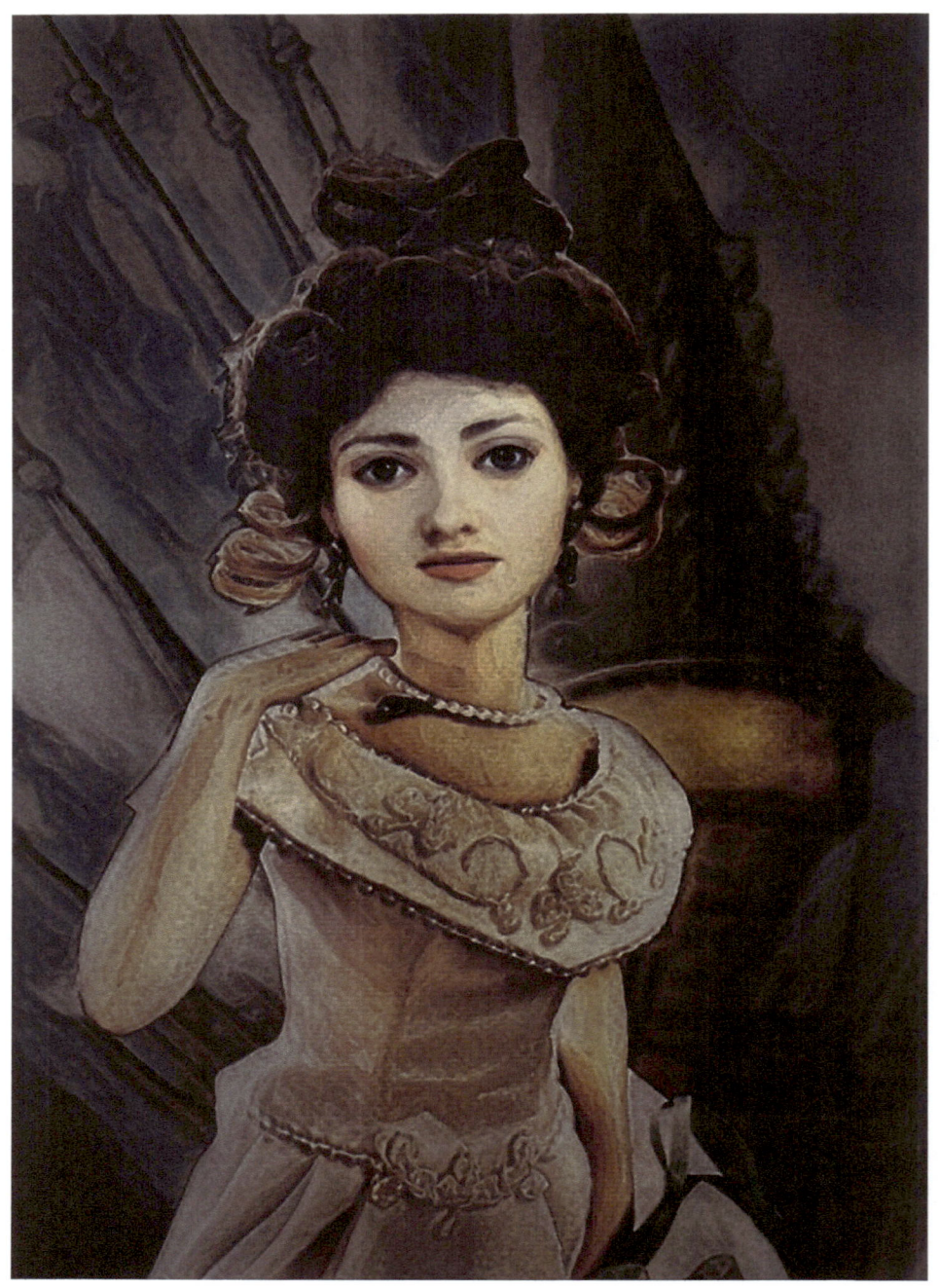

All I wanted:

Psalm of the Hyacinth

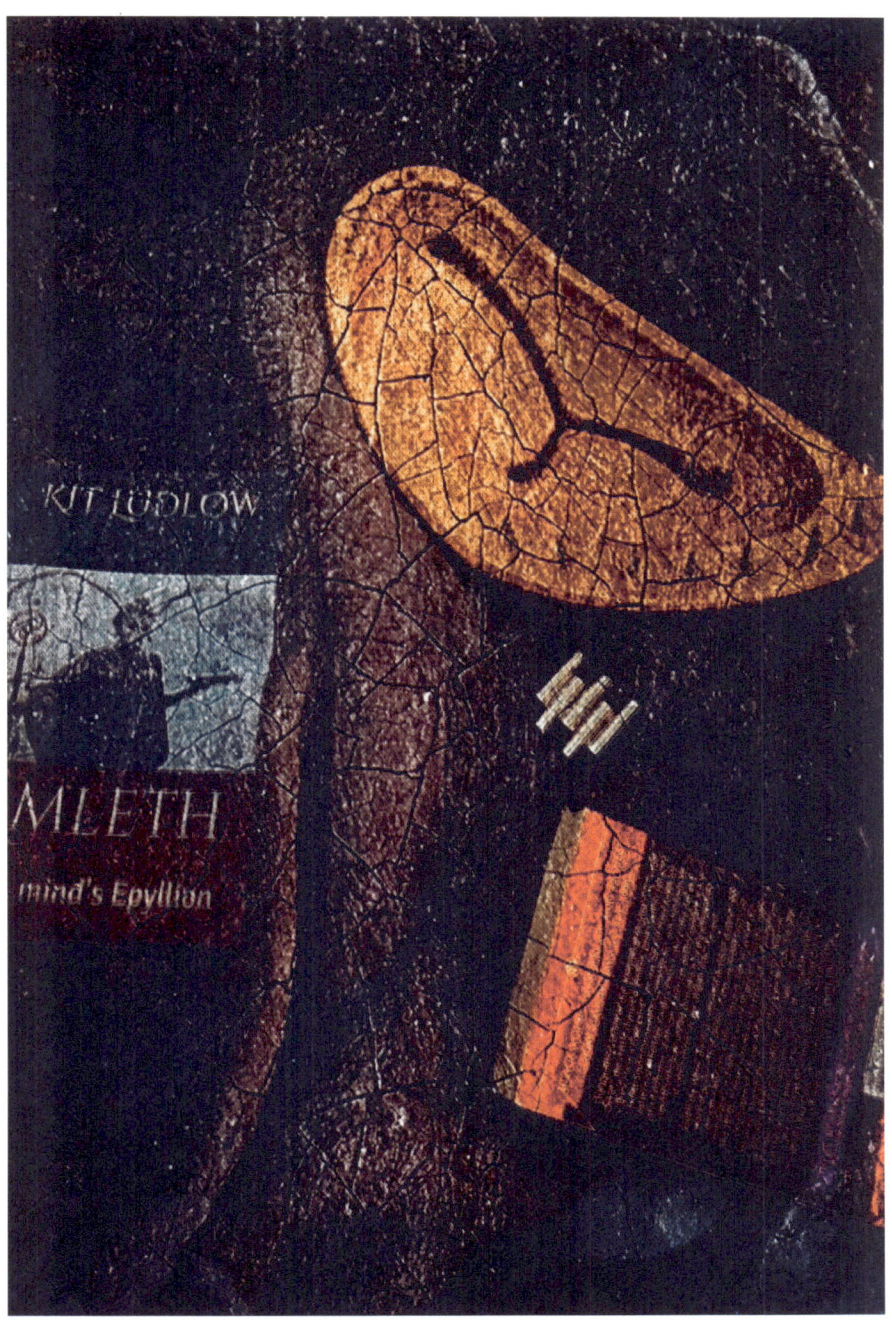

Notes of singing,

Psalm of the Hyacinth

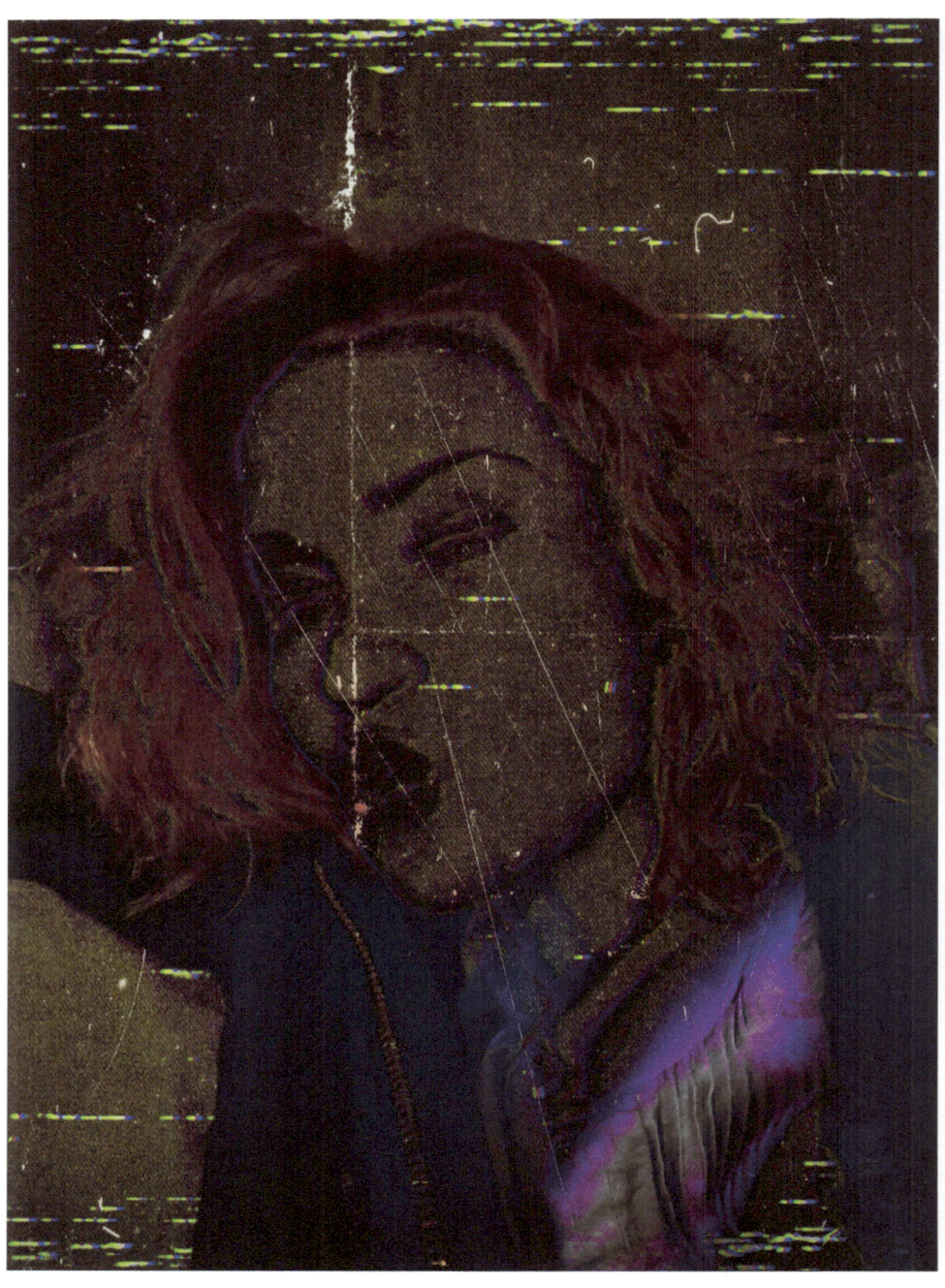

My song on the lips of many

Psalm of the Hyacinth

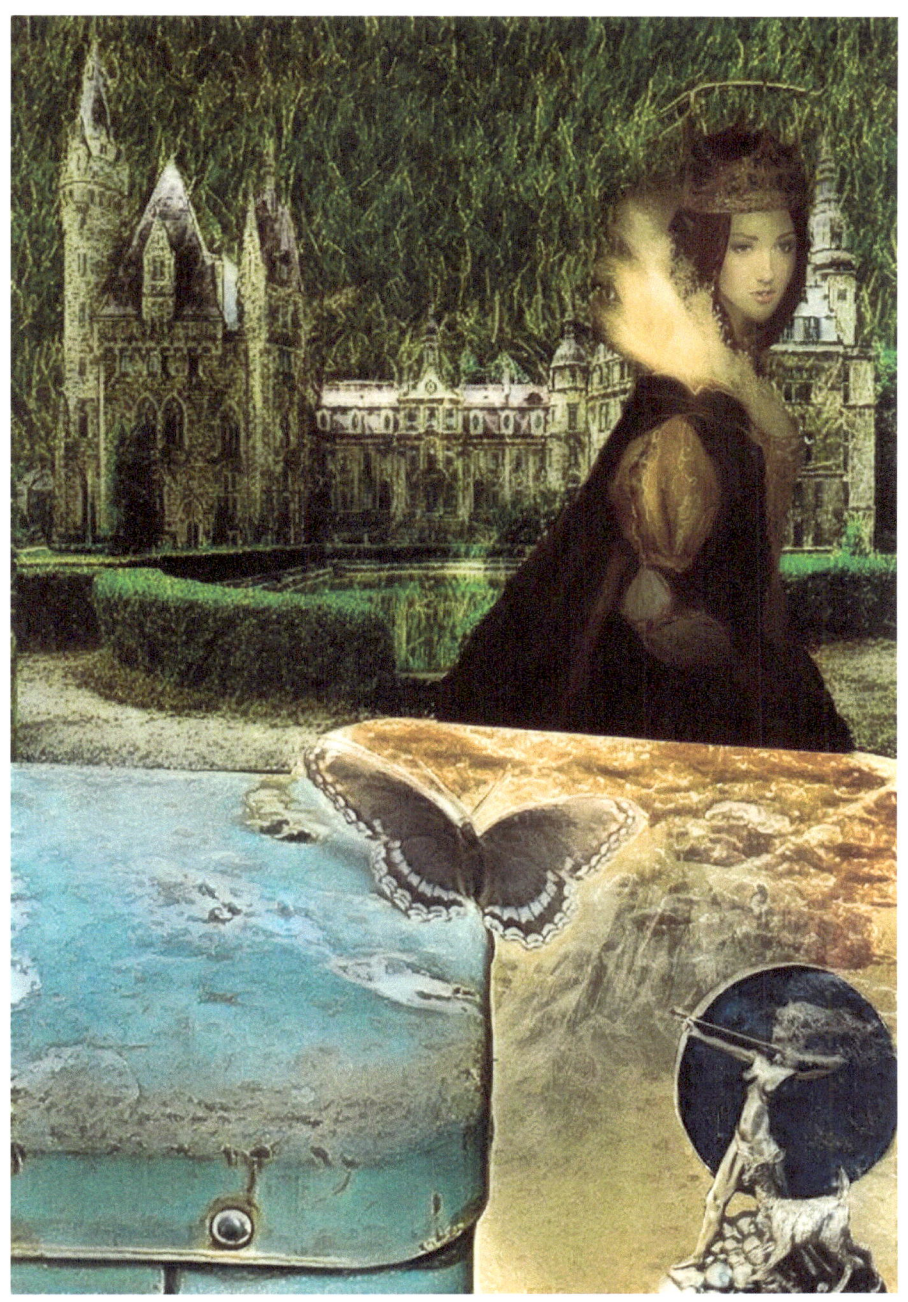

And you to witness the passion;

Psalm of the Hyacinth

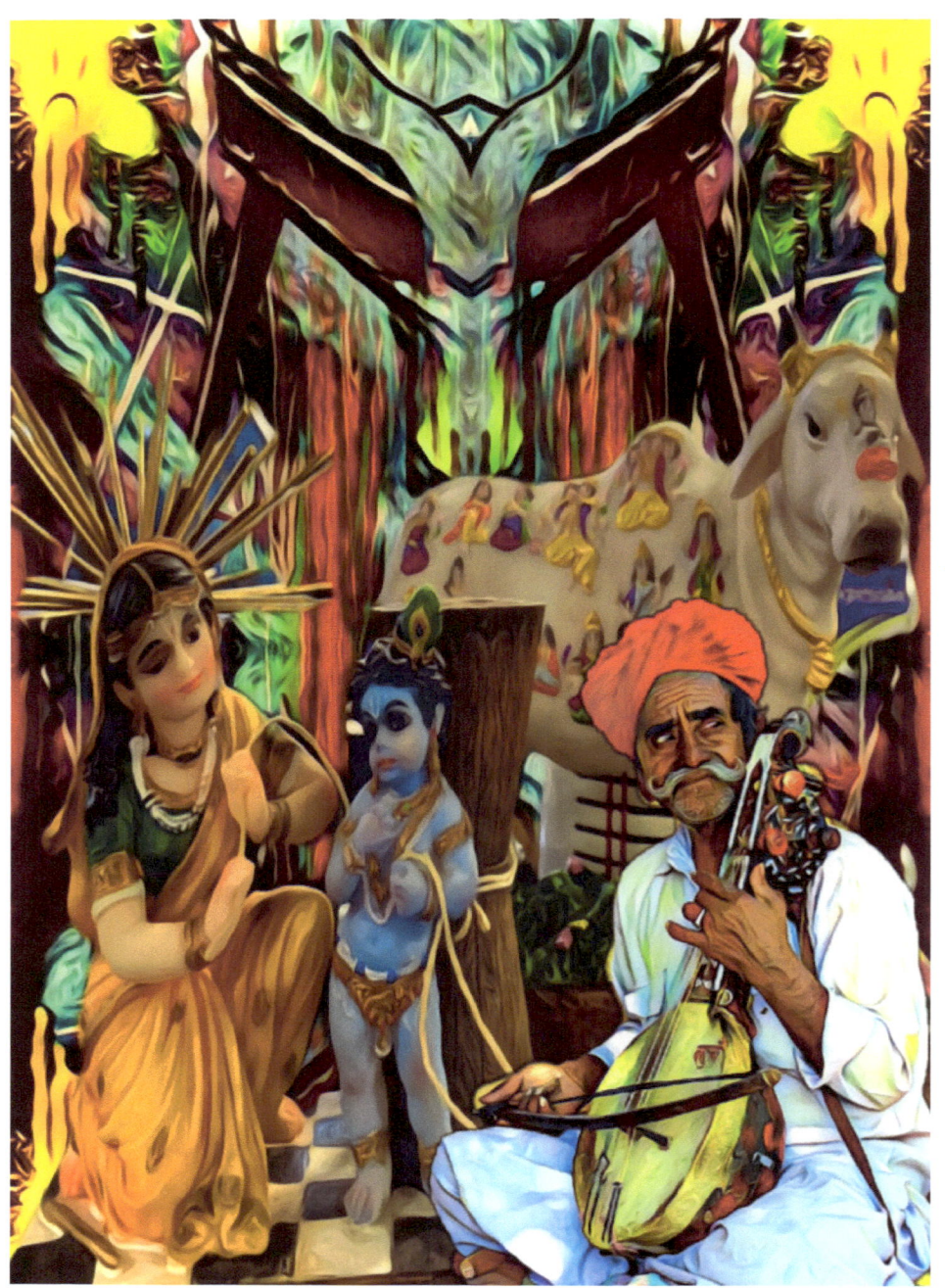

The madness heard in a chorus.

Psalm of the Hyacinth

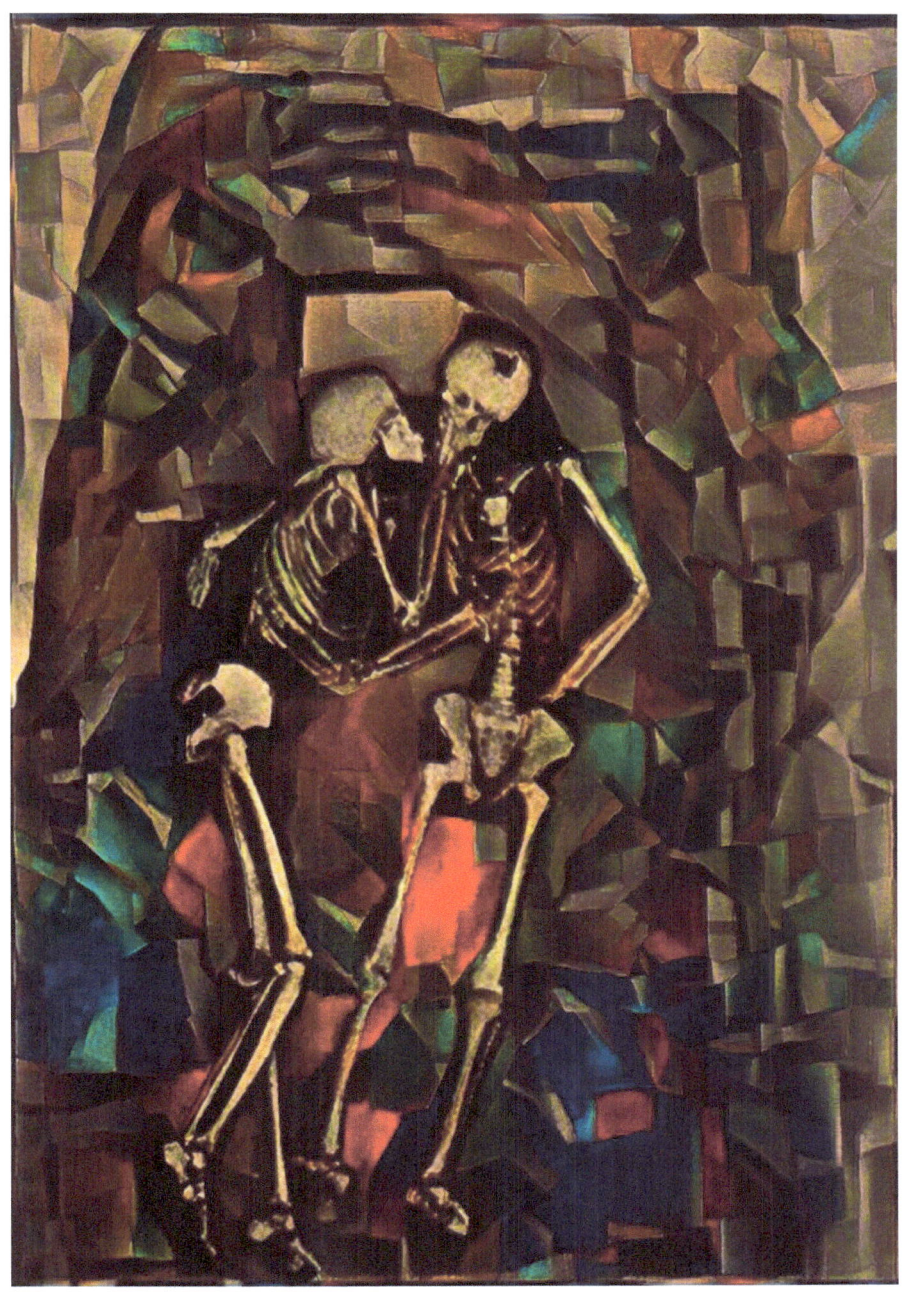

Long after the flesh has ashen,

Psalm of the Hyacinth

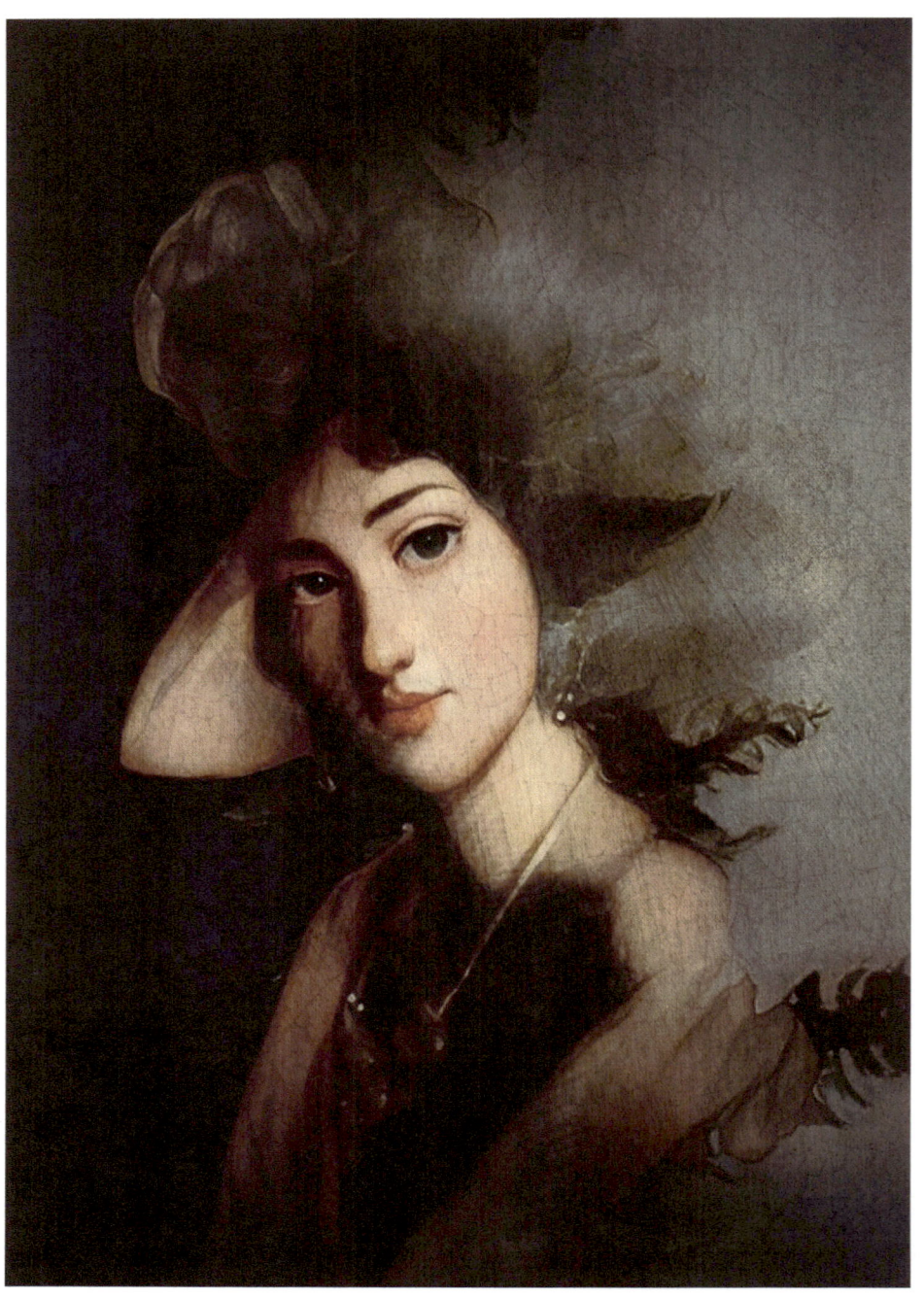

Long lives a memory for us-

Psalm of the Hyacinth

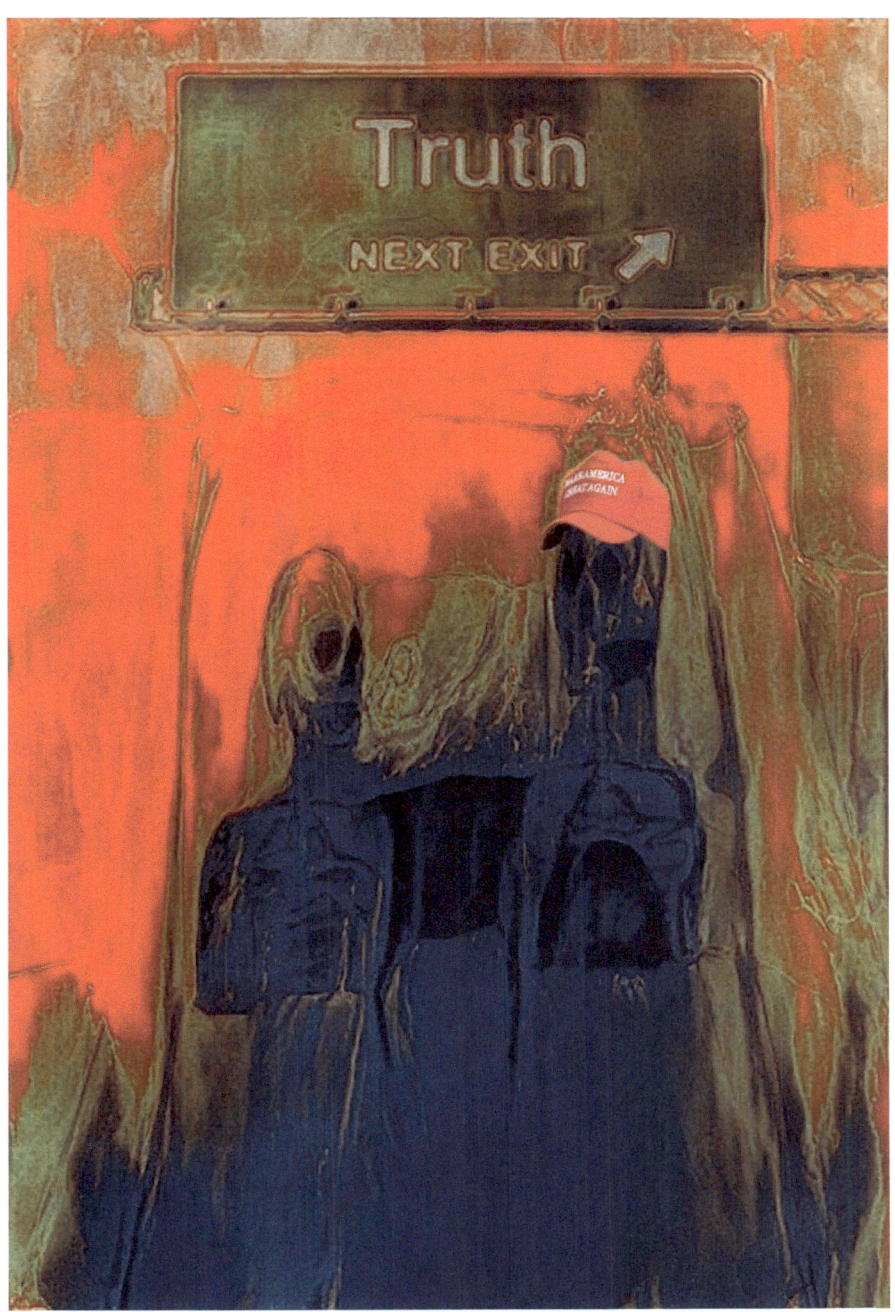

The trauma of harsh chords in pitch,

Psalm of the Hyacinth

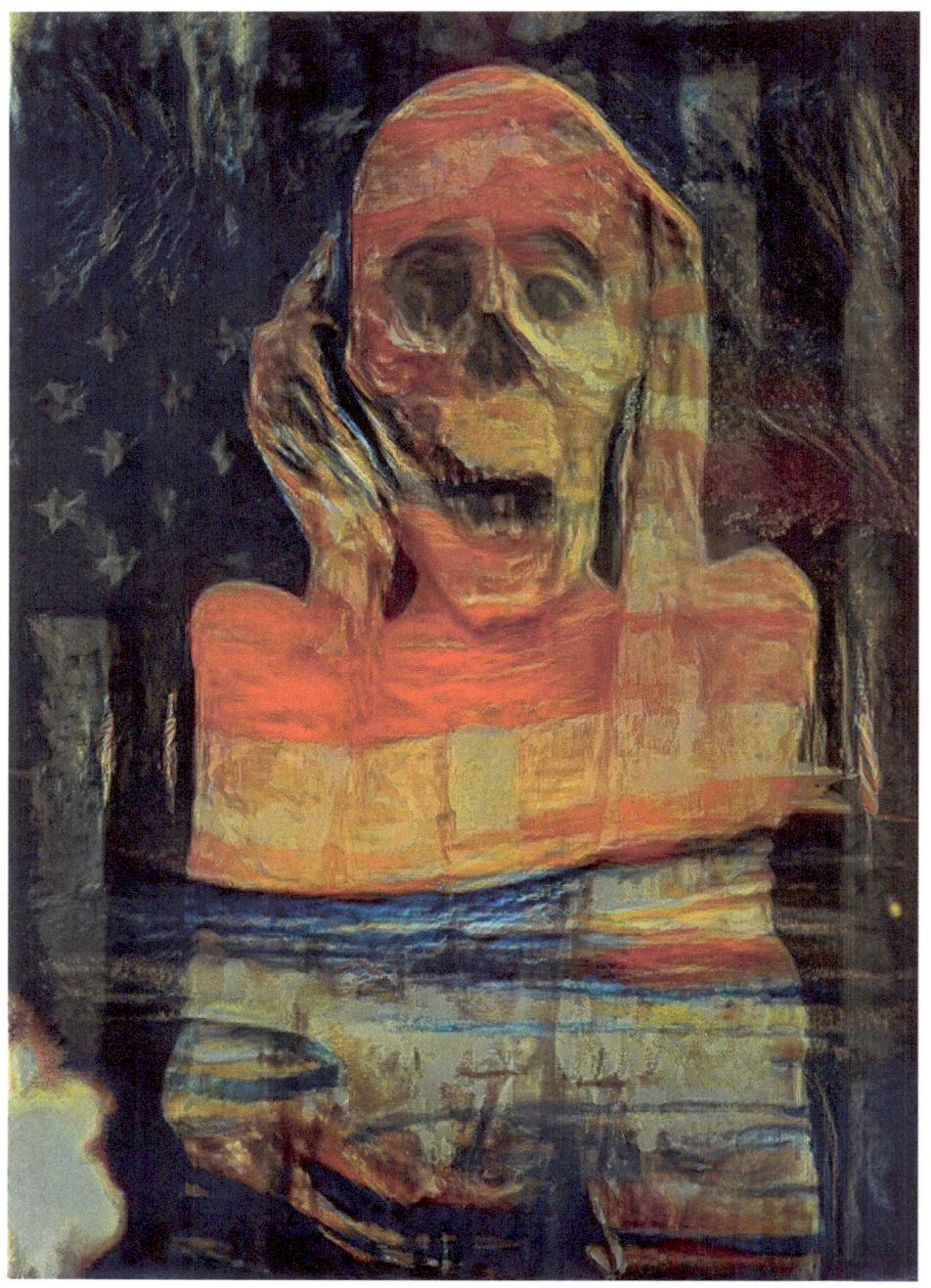

The off-rhythm pulse of our thoughts.

Psalm of the Hyacinth

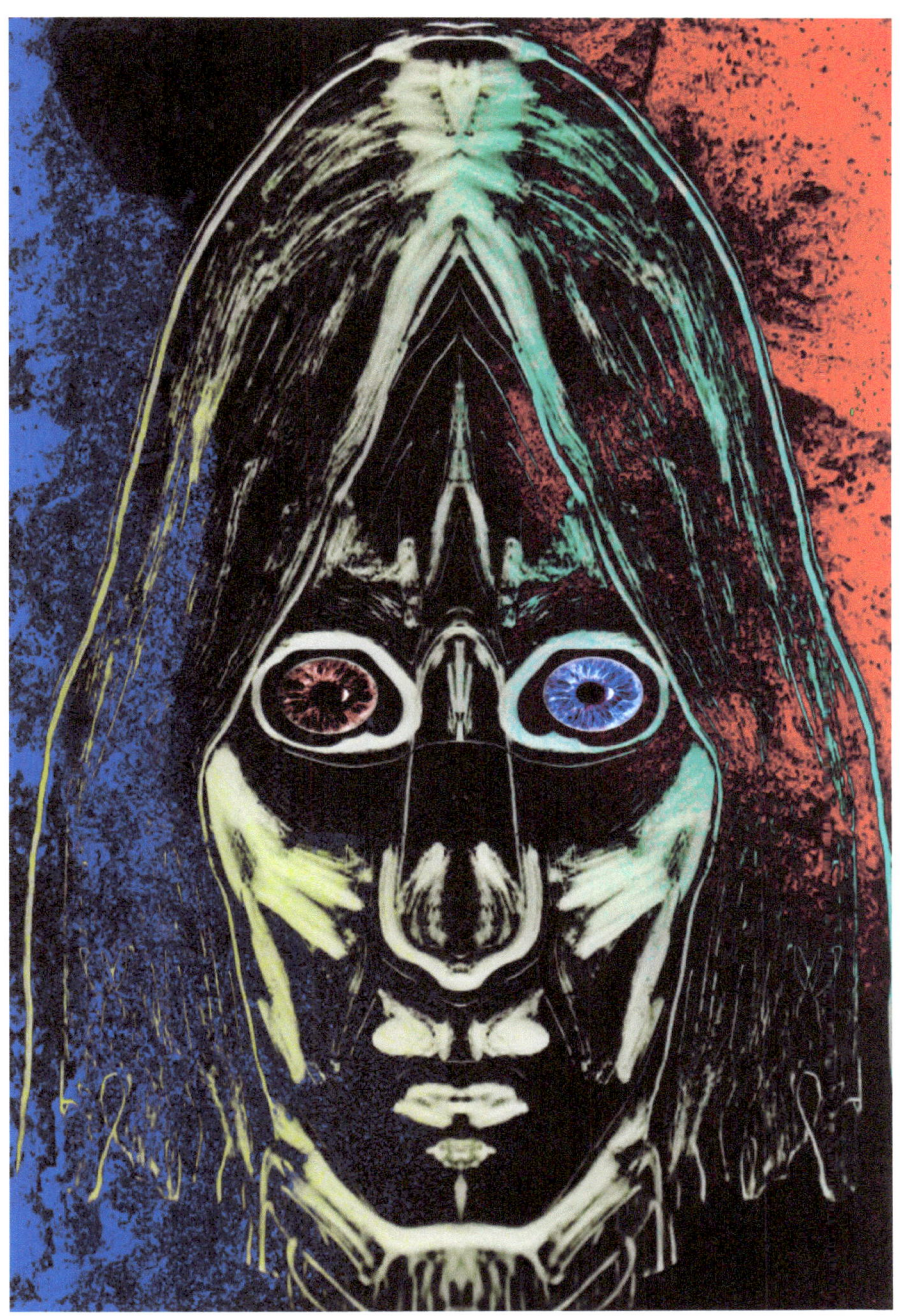

Voodoo doll in need of a stitch:

Psalm of the Hyacinth

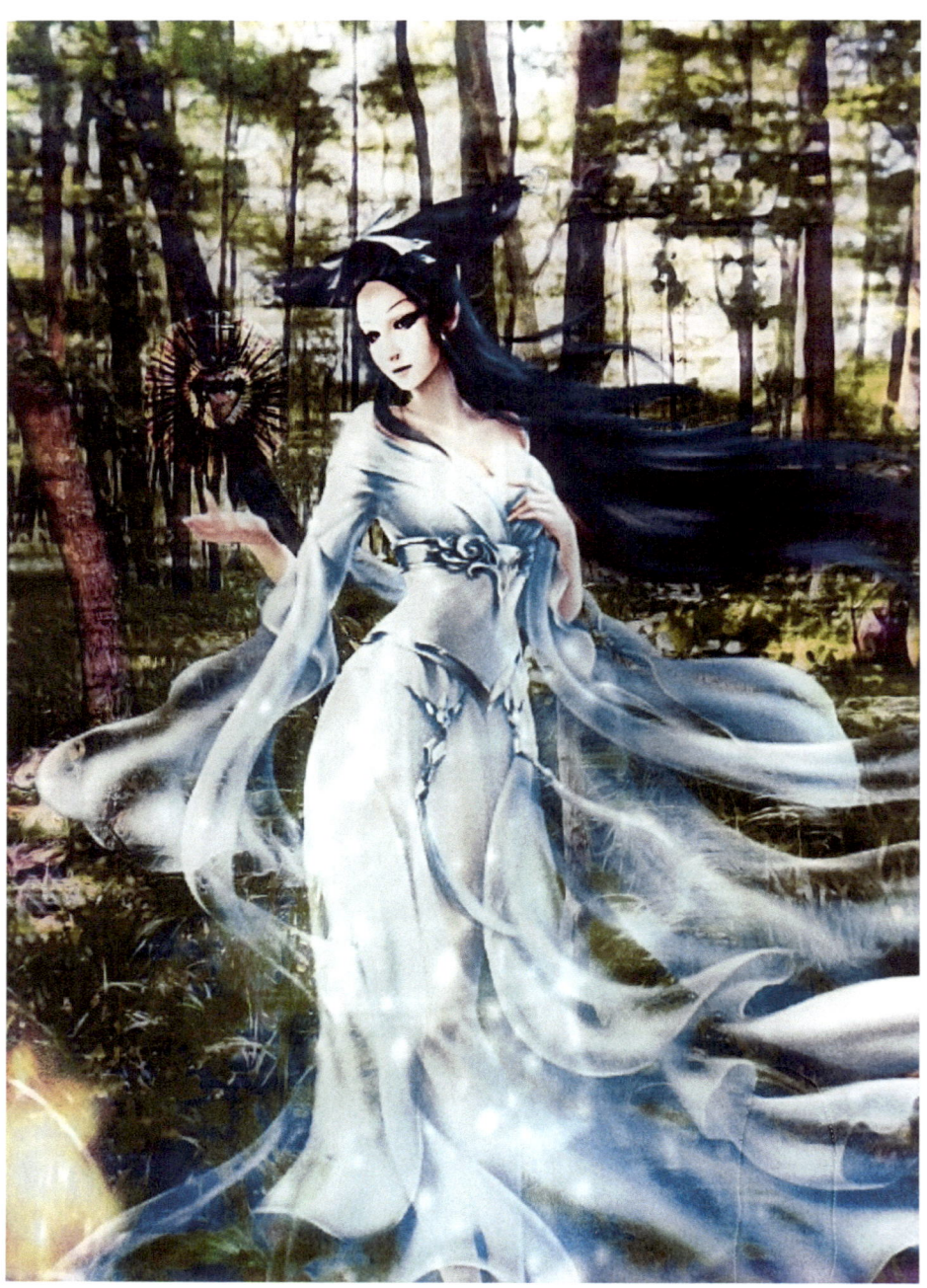

Fate's pin and needles can't be bought.

Psalm of the Hyacinth

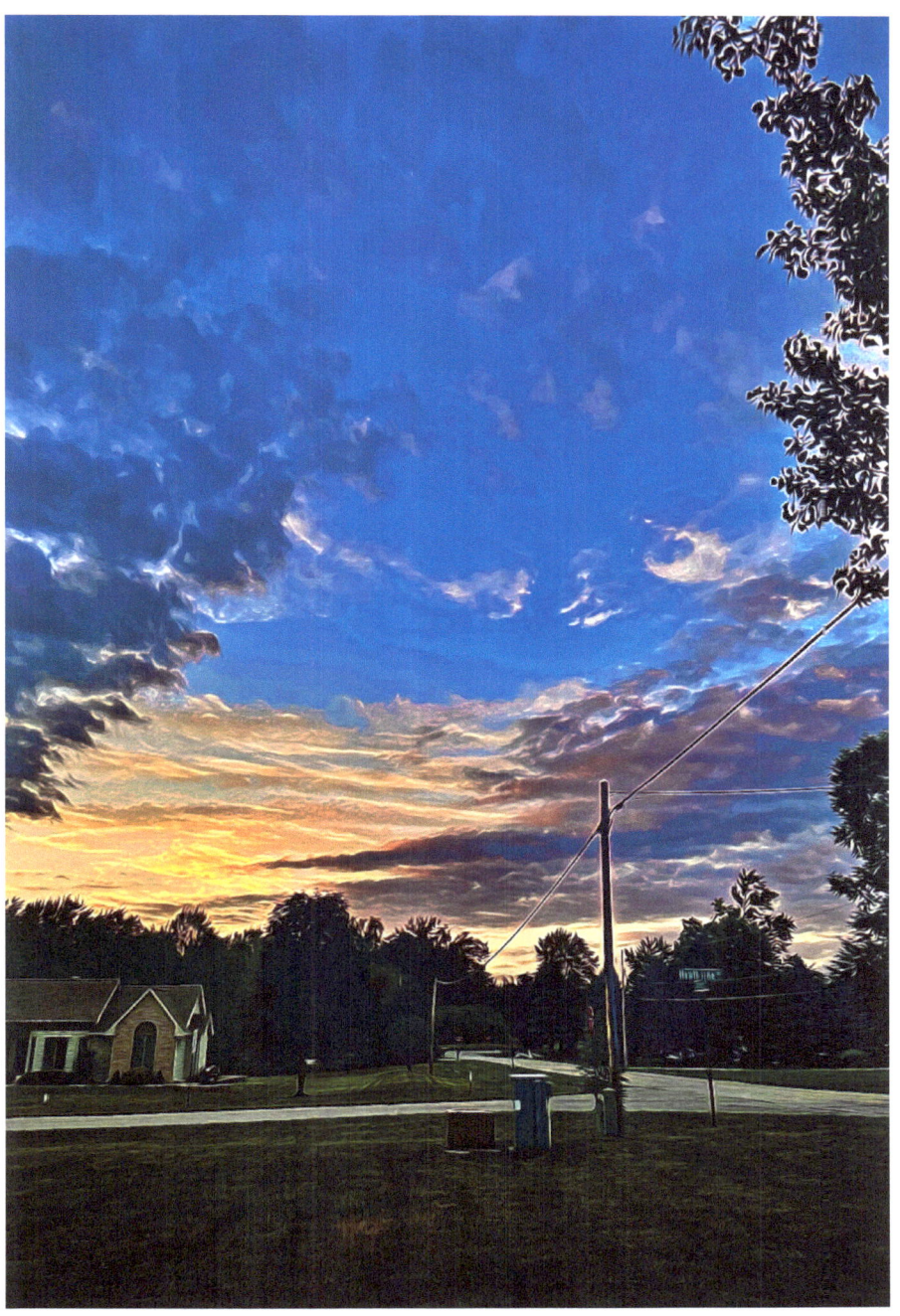

I left my threads in the labyrinth;

Psalm of the Hyacinth

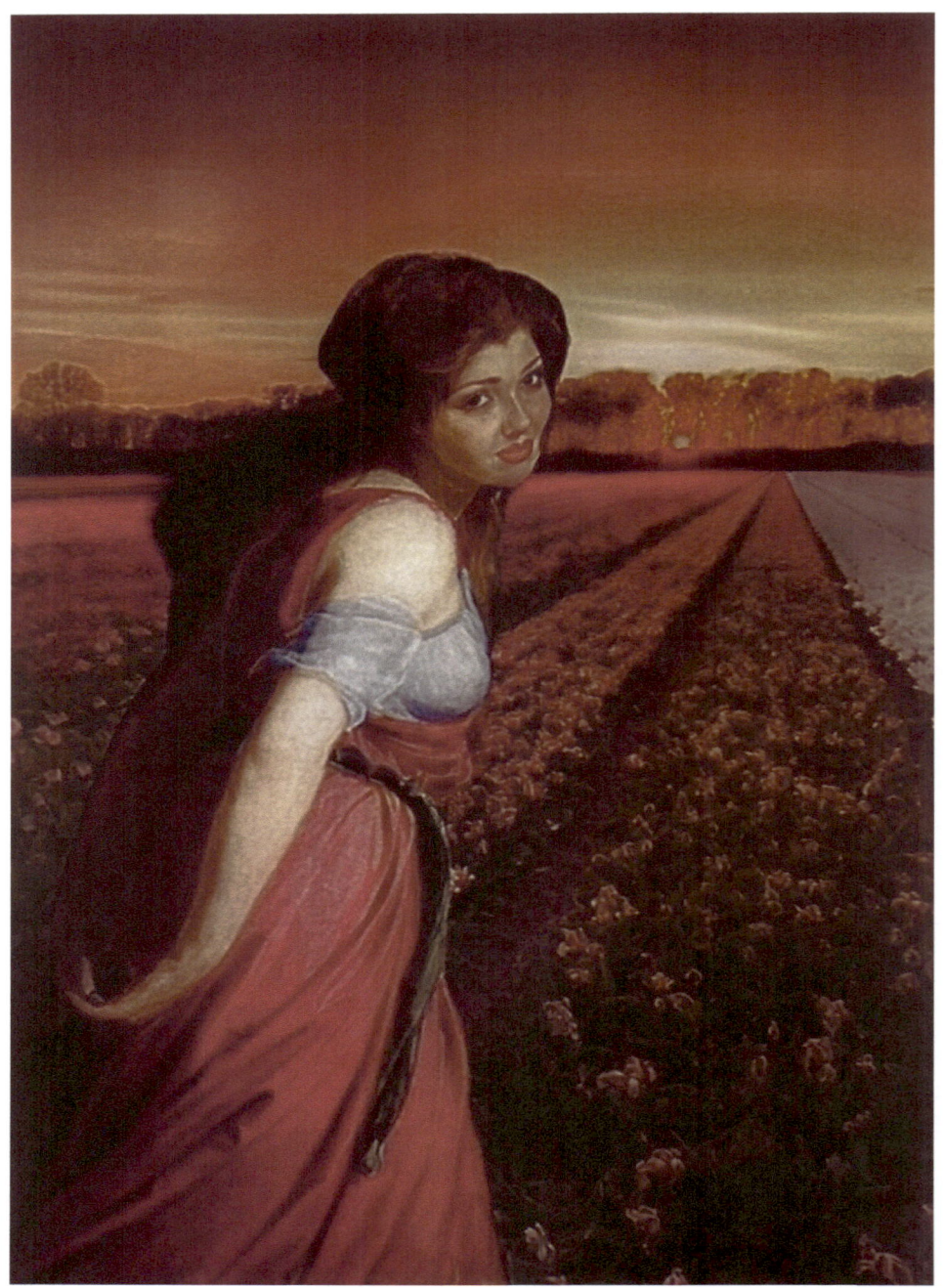

Please follow them,

Psalm of the Hyacinth

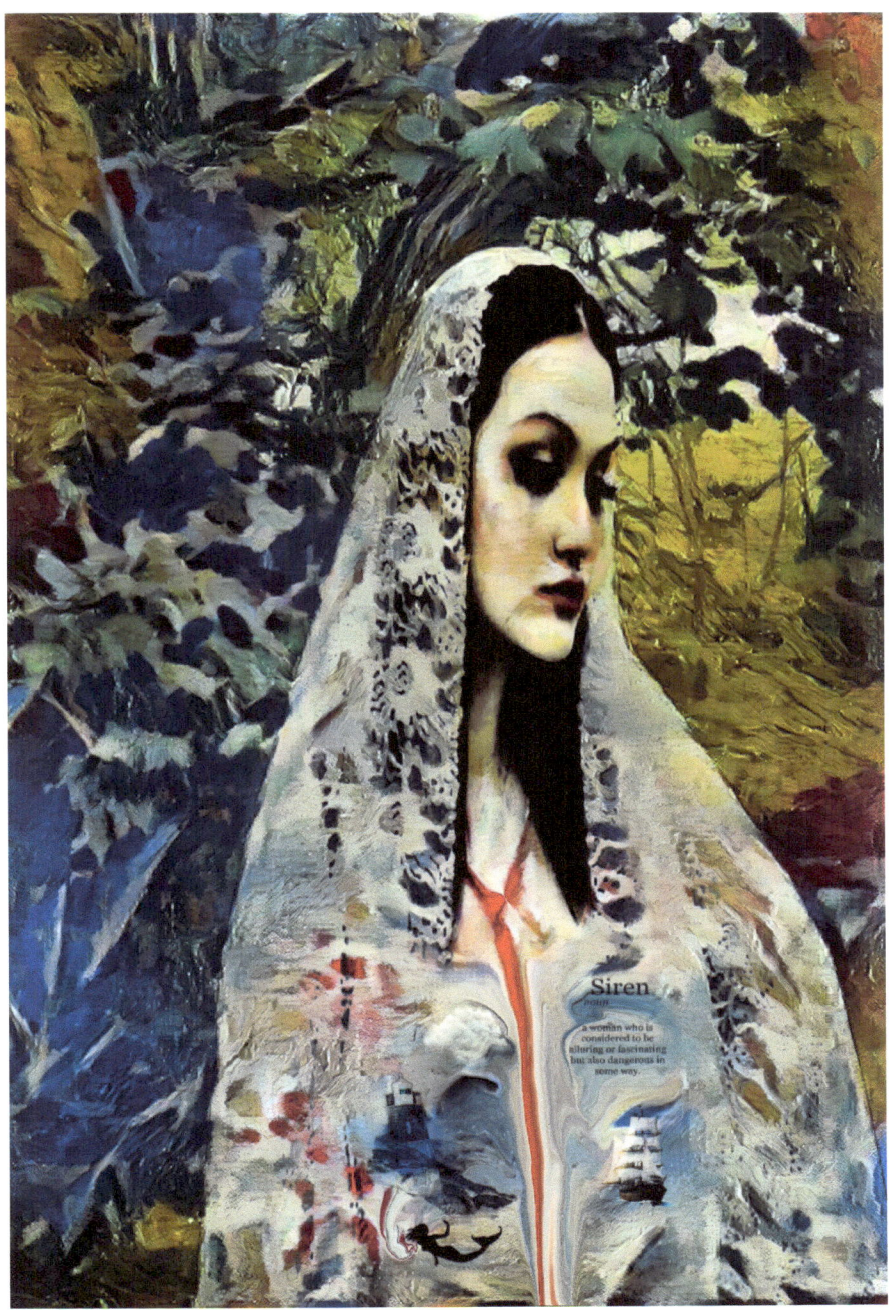

My hyacinth.

Psalm of the Hyacinth

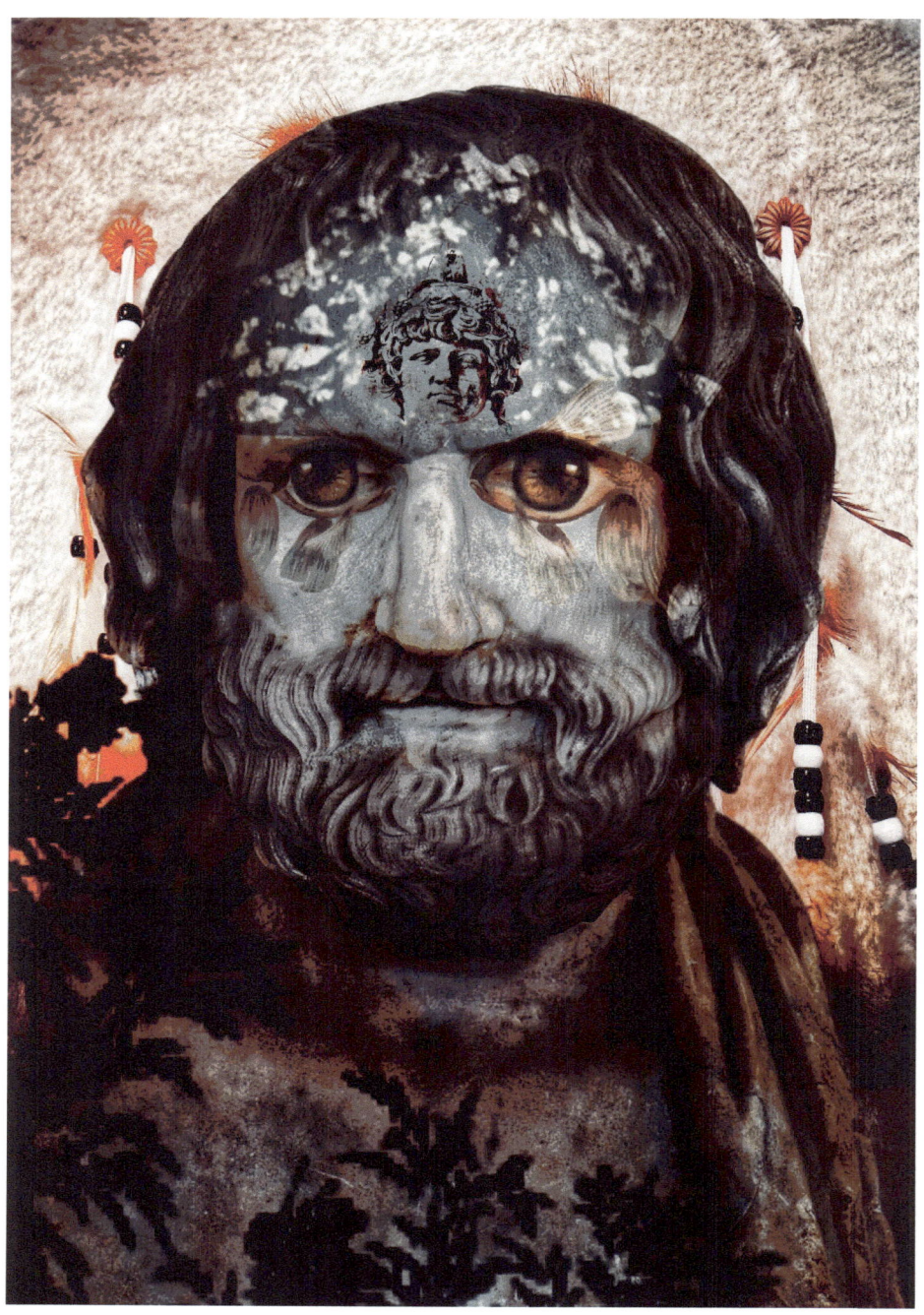

Like Euripides in a cave,

Psalm of the Hyacinth

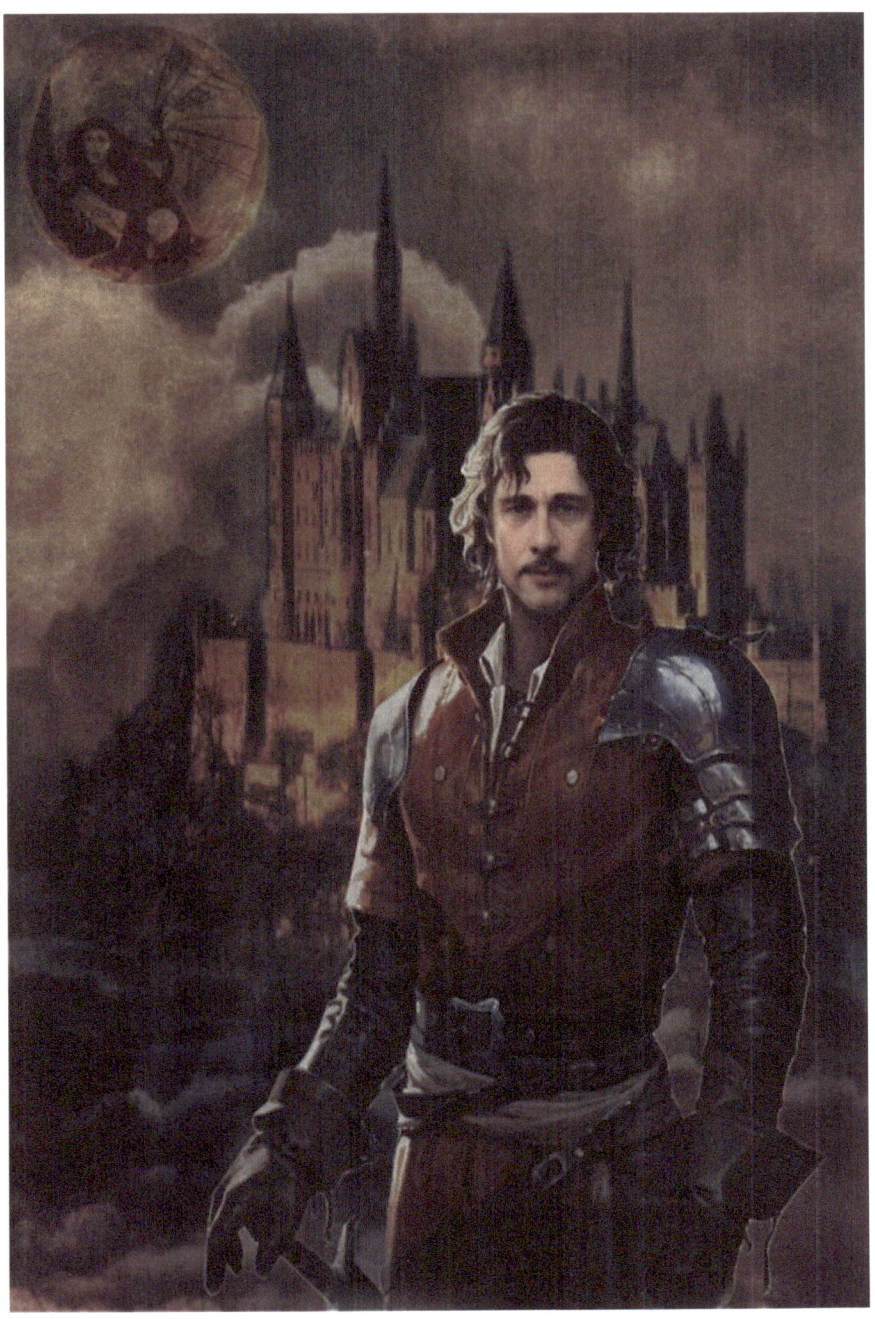

Composing goat odes of torture,

Psalm of the Hyacinth

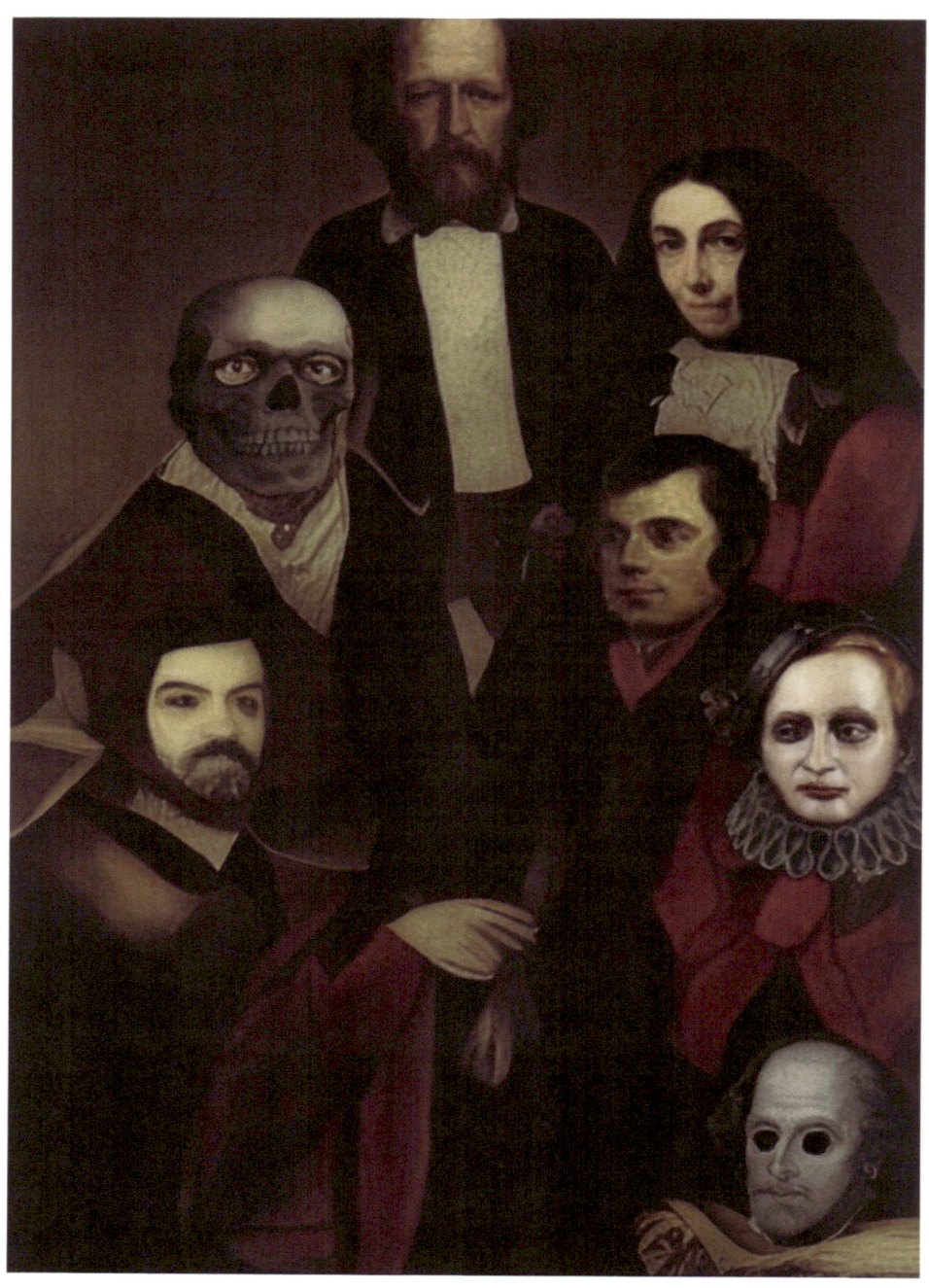

Or De Vere lost in masquerade,

Psalm of the Hyacinth

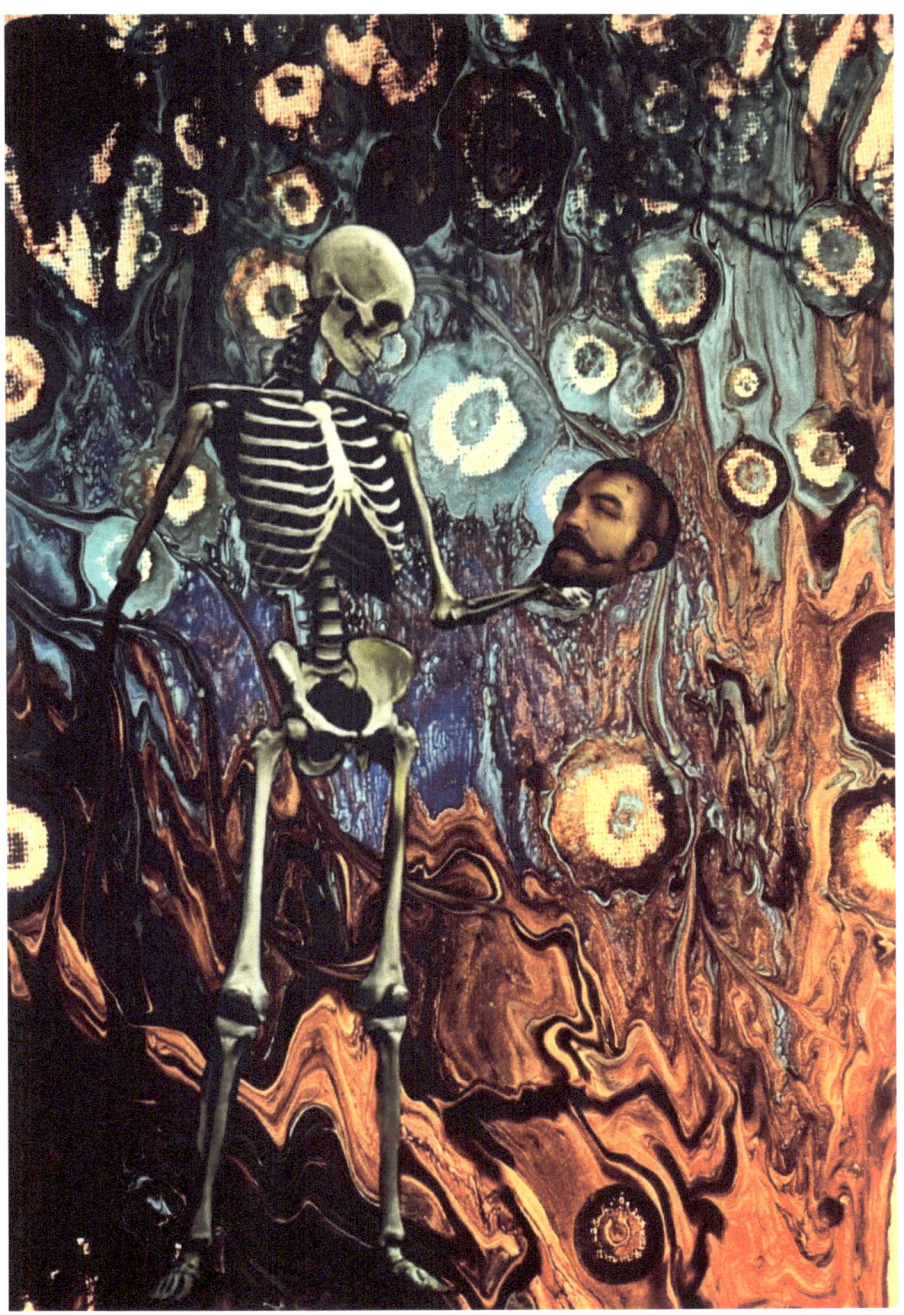

Spear-shaking the loss of nature,

Psalm of the Hyacinth

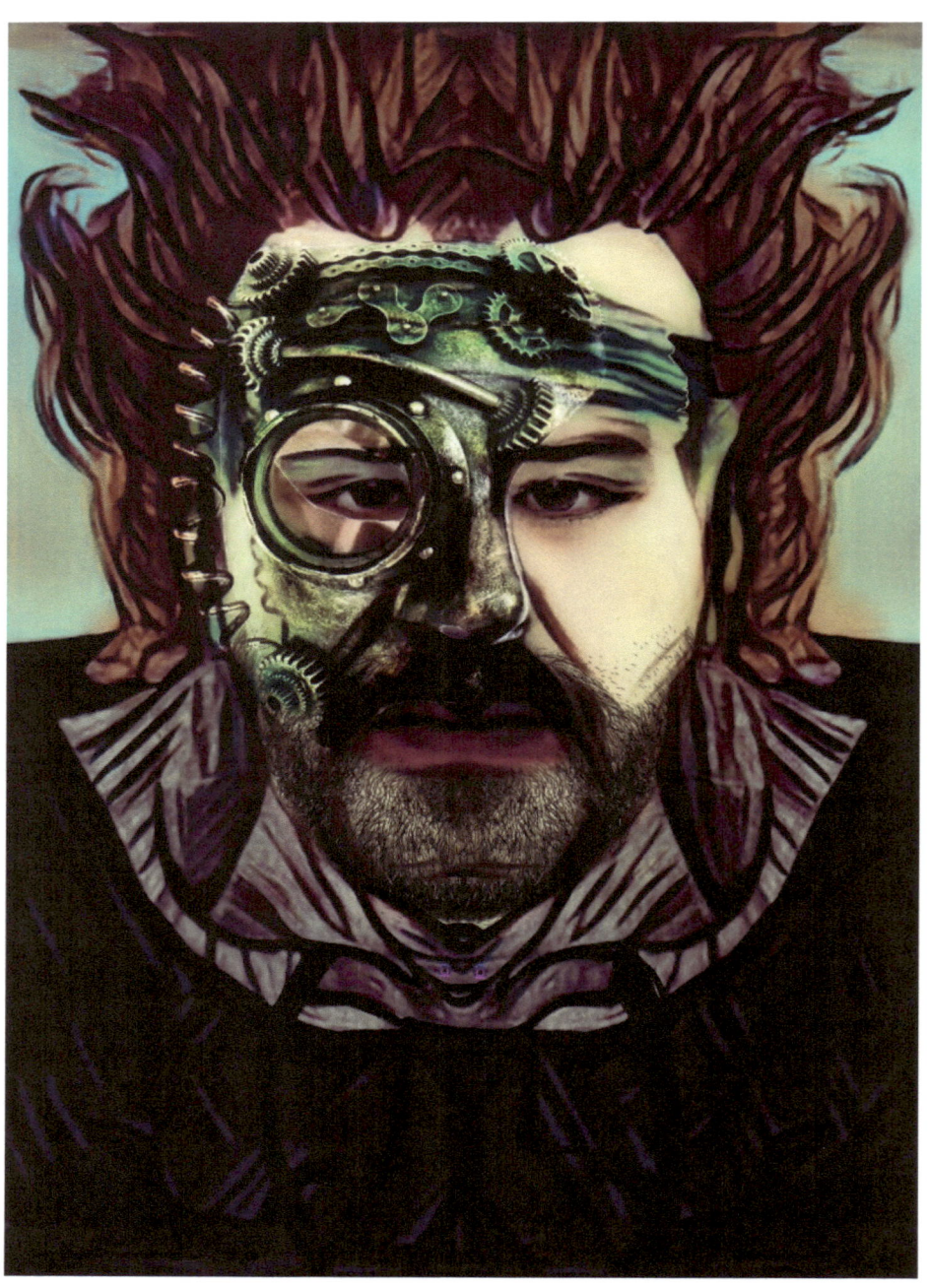

I perform my part for the stage.

Psalm of the Hyacinth

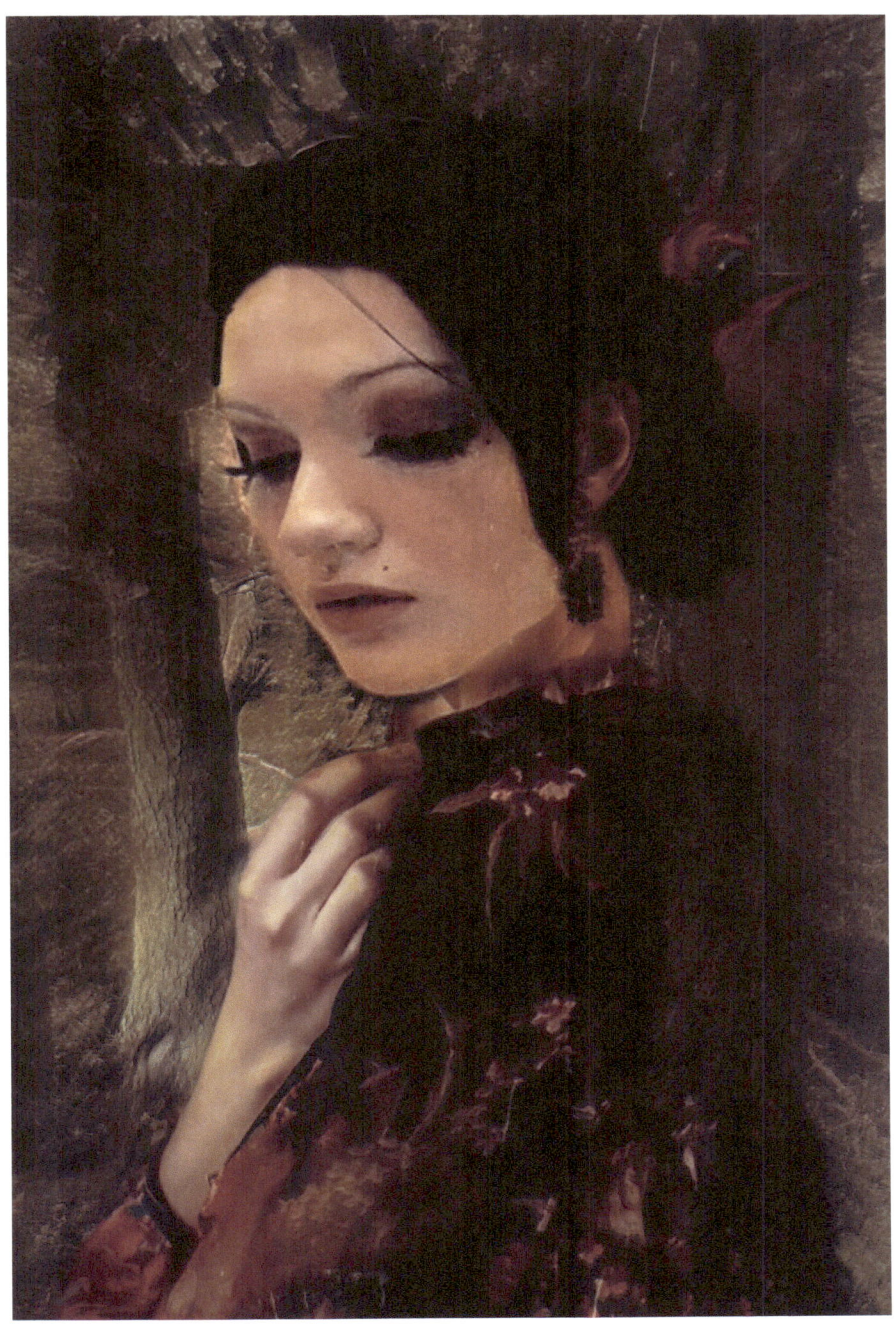

You say the lines,

Psalm of the Hyacinth

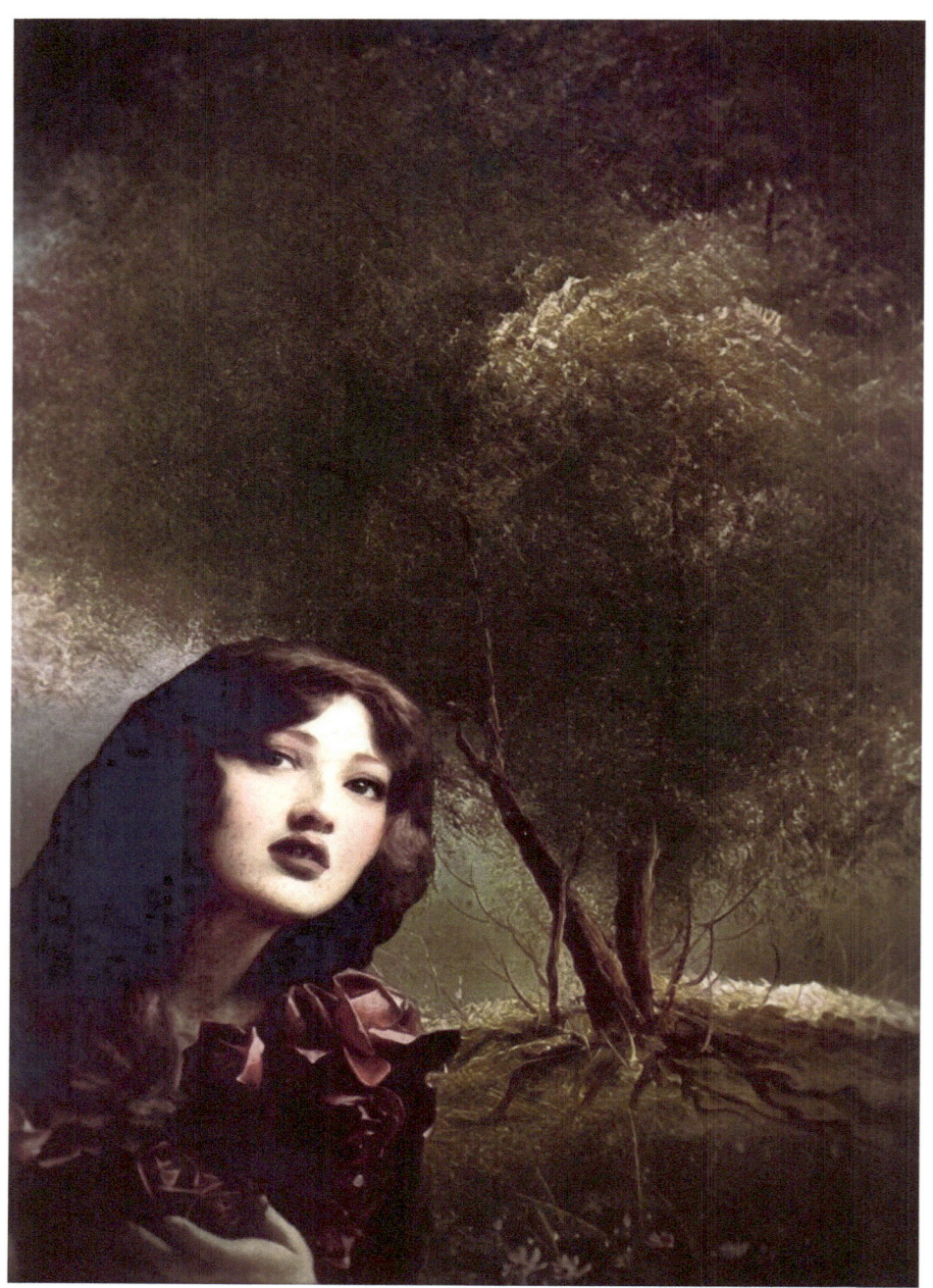

Full of rhythm,

Psalm of the Hyacinth

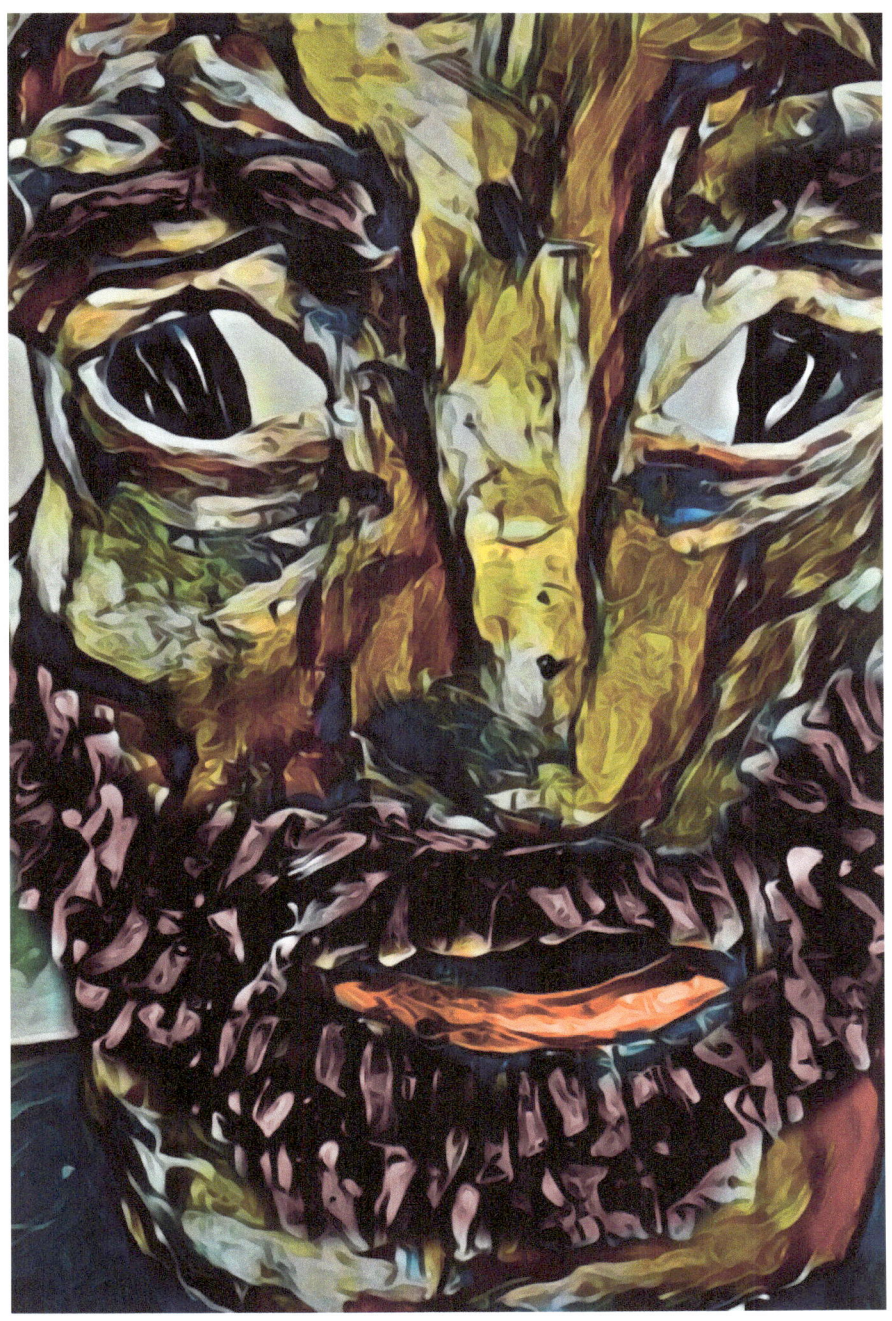

Storm through the stress,

Psalm of the Hyacinth

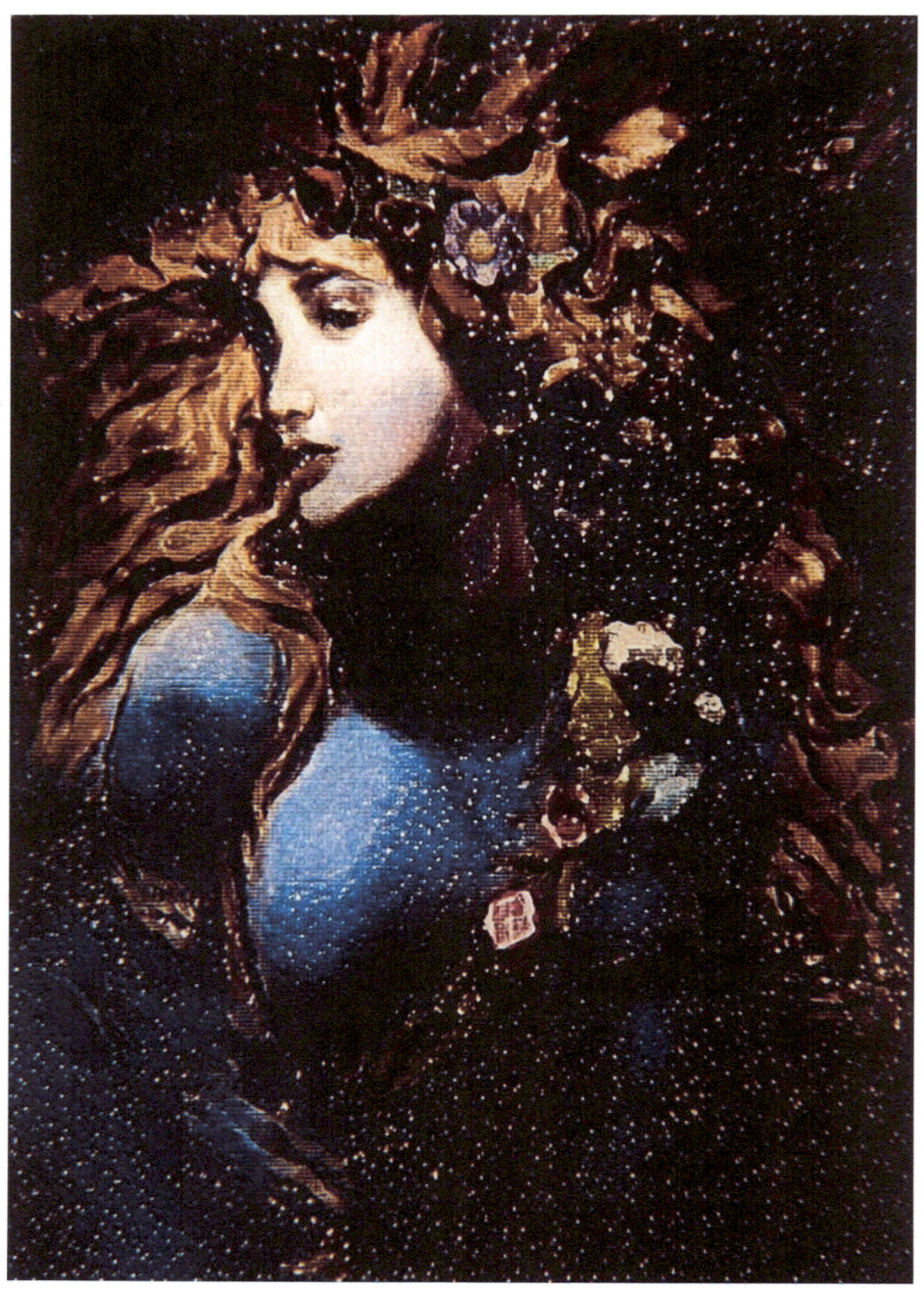

Secret in sage.

Psalm of the Hyacinth

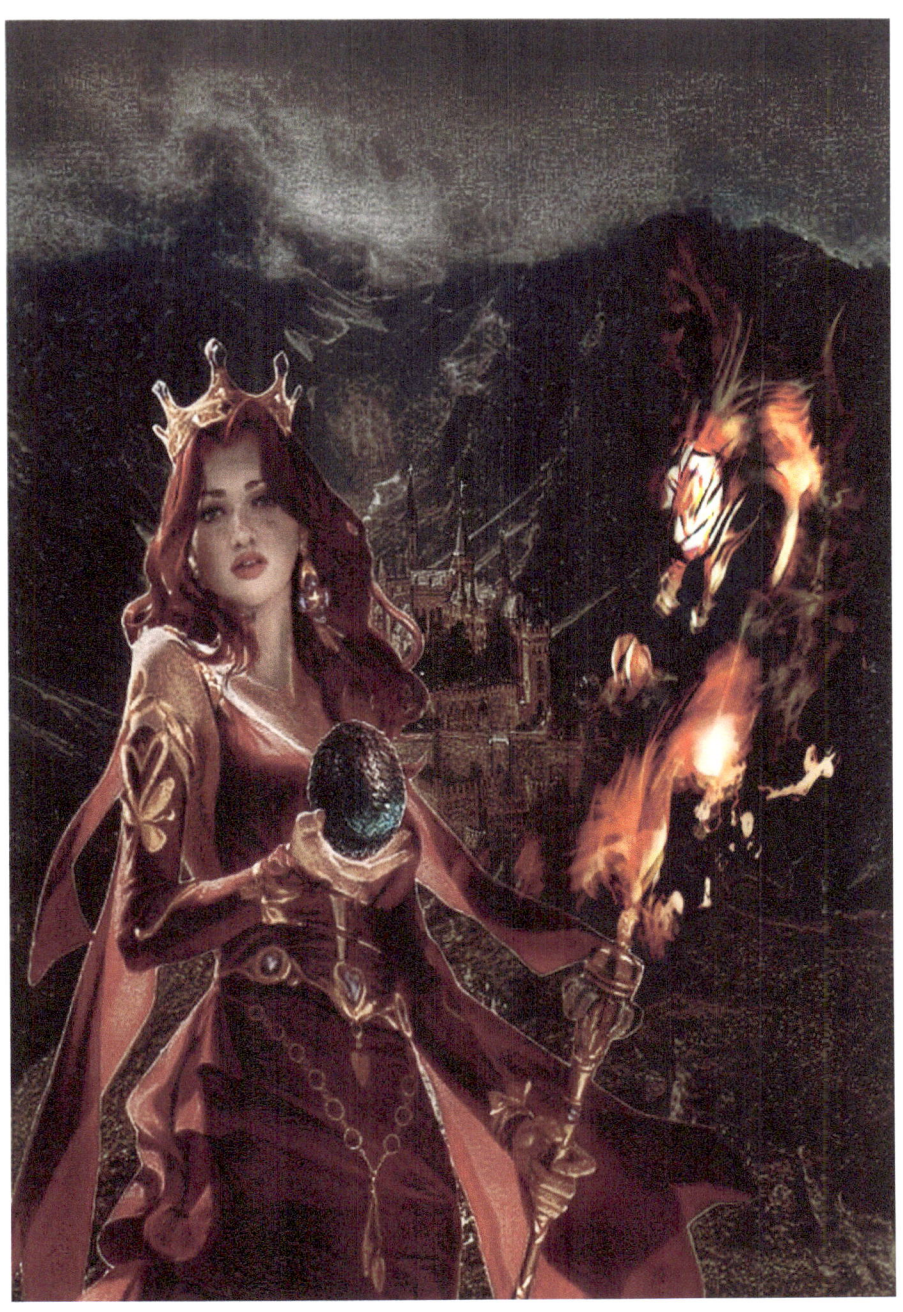

Be an Oracle but rid phlegm,

Psalm of the Hyacinth

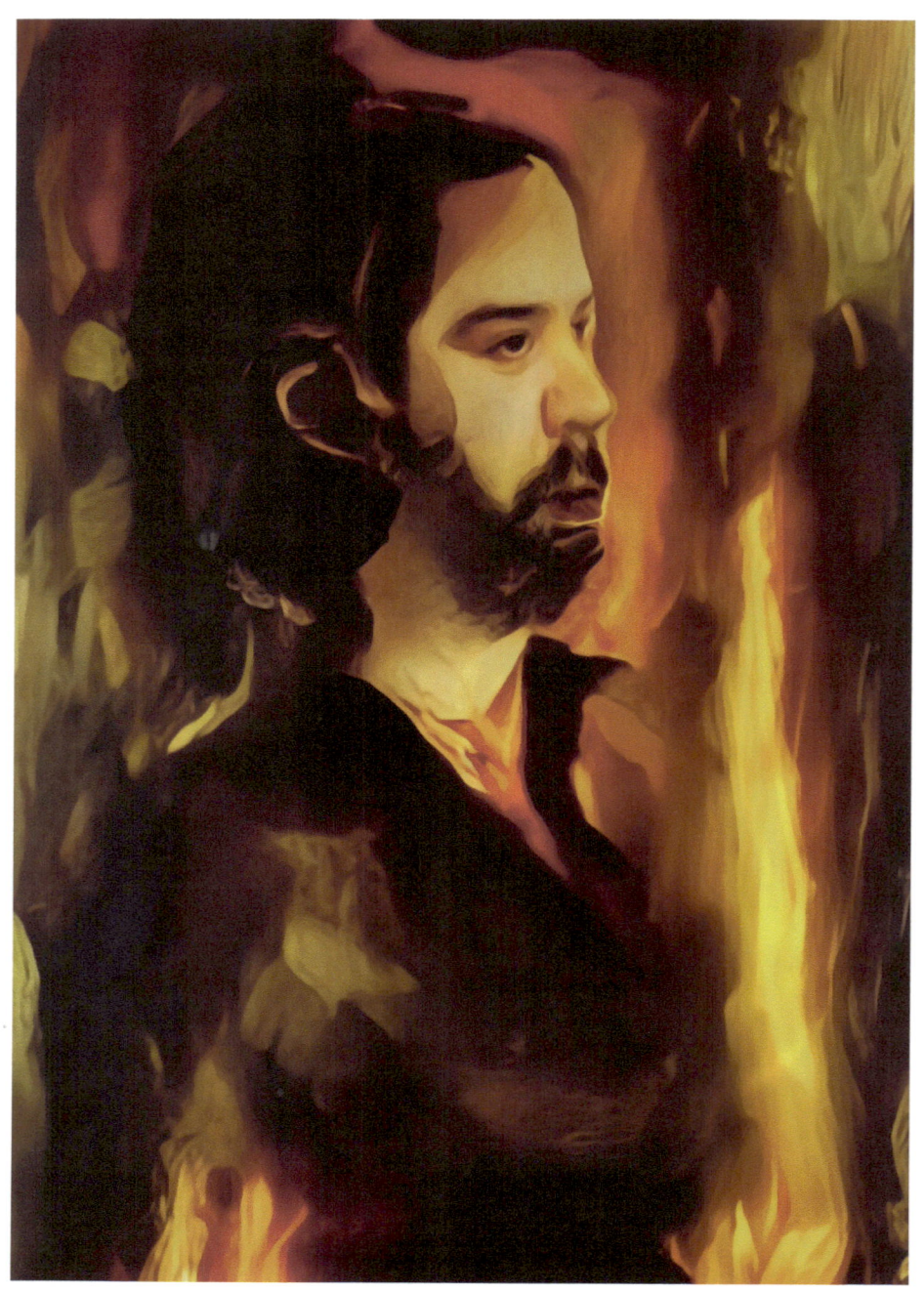

The settled state of apathy,

Psalm of the Hyacinth

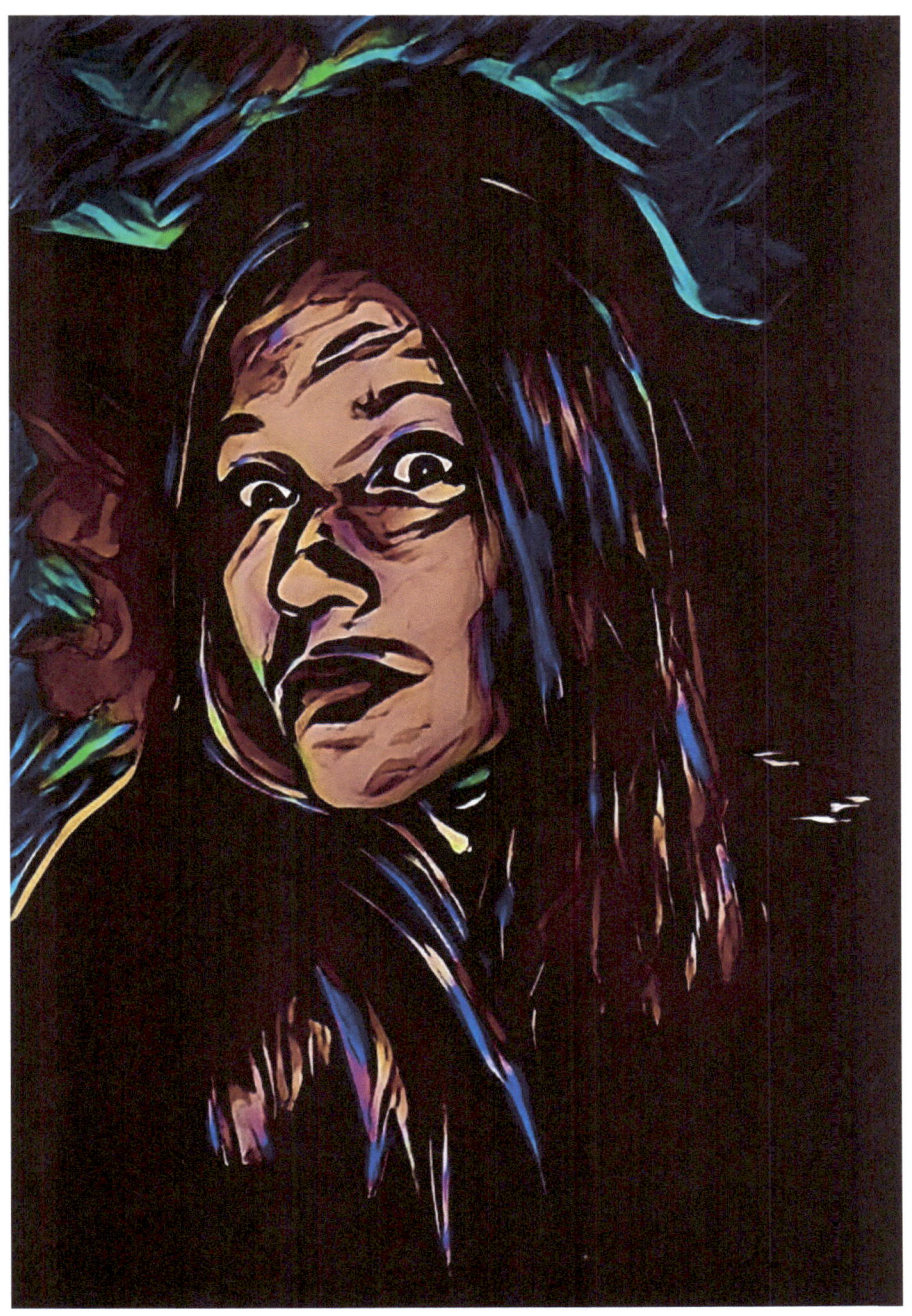

And foretell futures with taboo.

Psalm of the Hyacinth

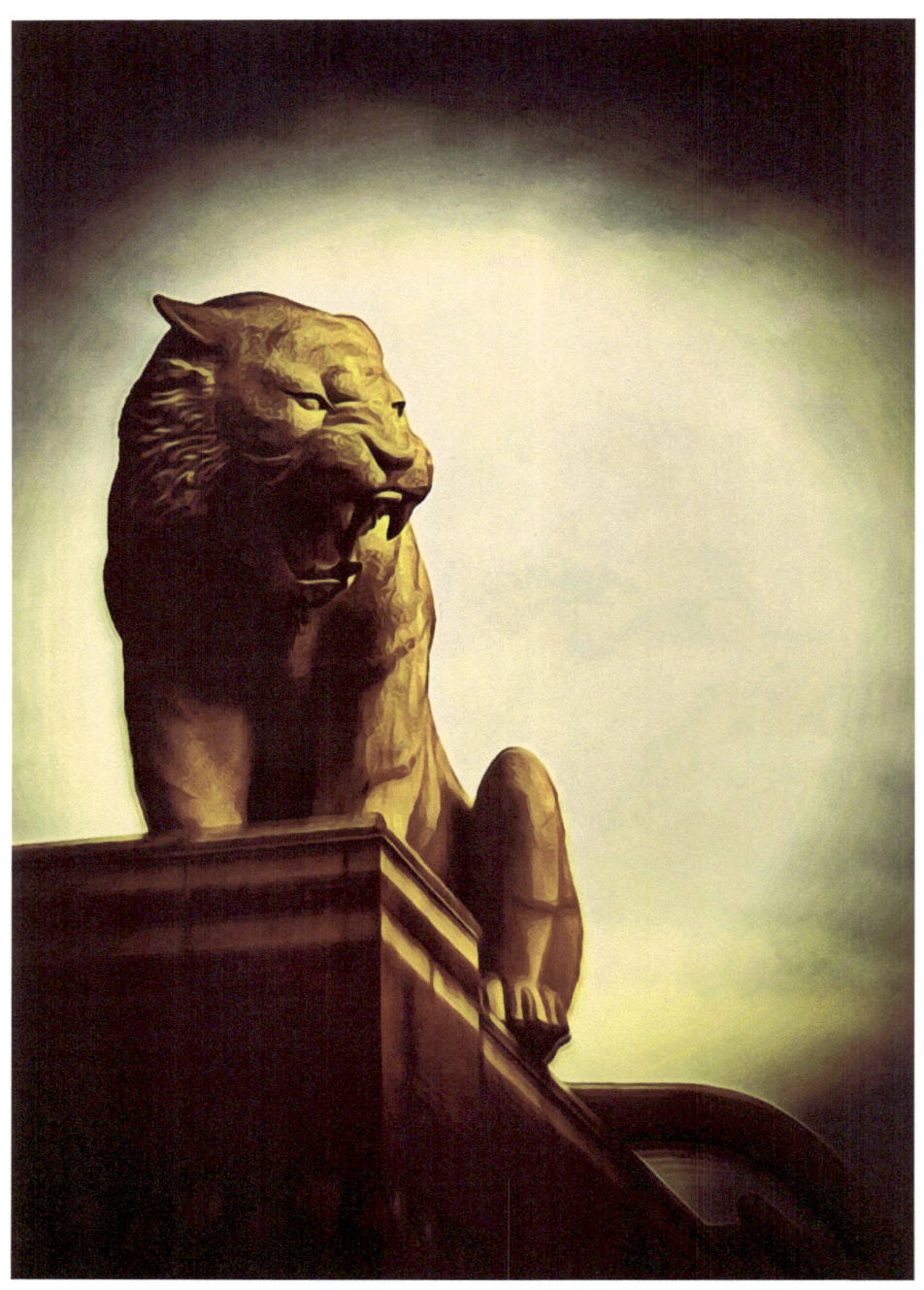

Here cast in bronze,

Psalm of the Hyacinth

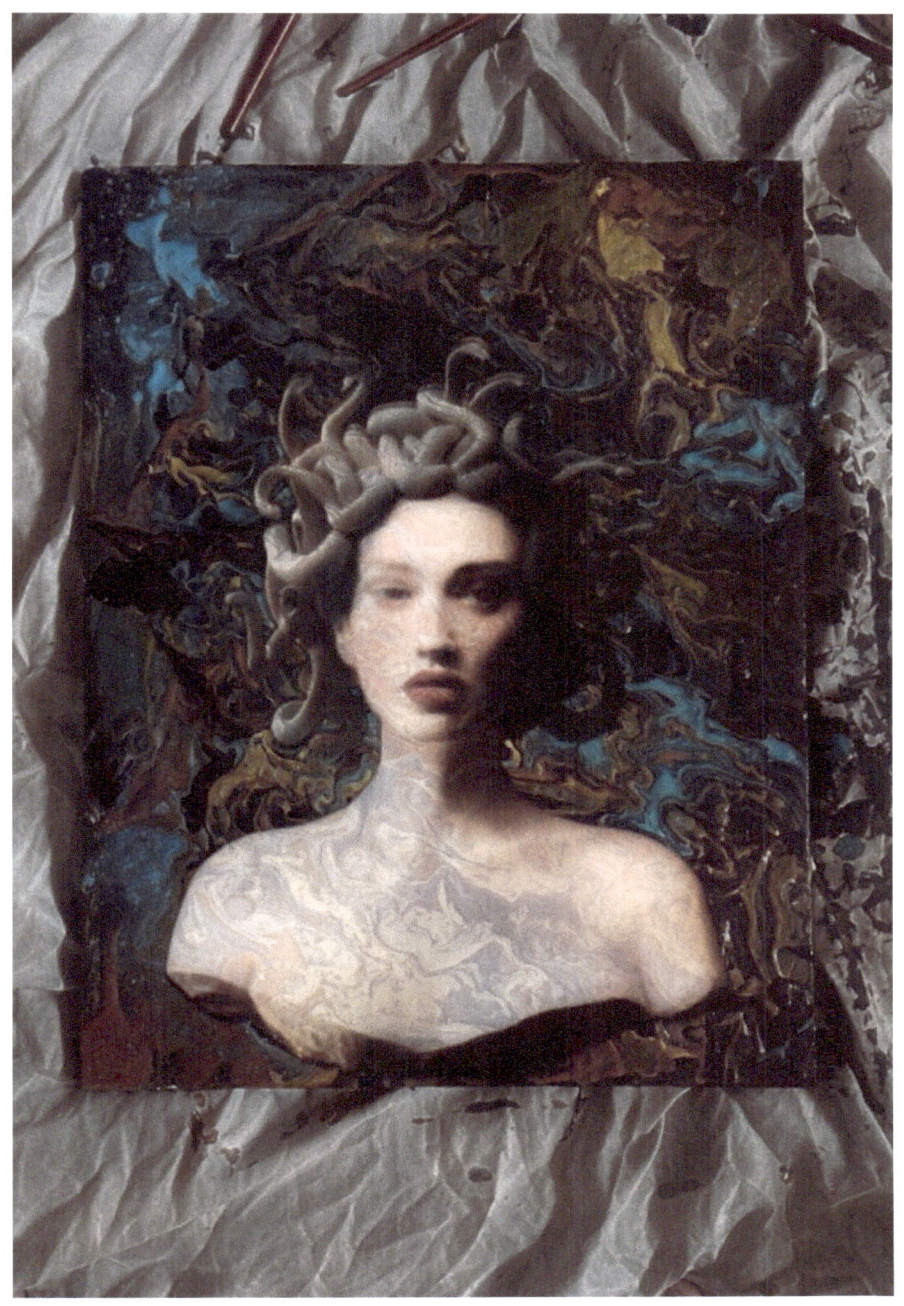

Patina green,

Psalm of the Hyacinth

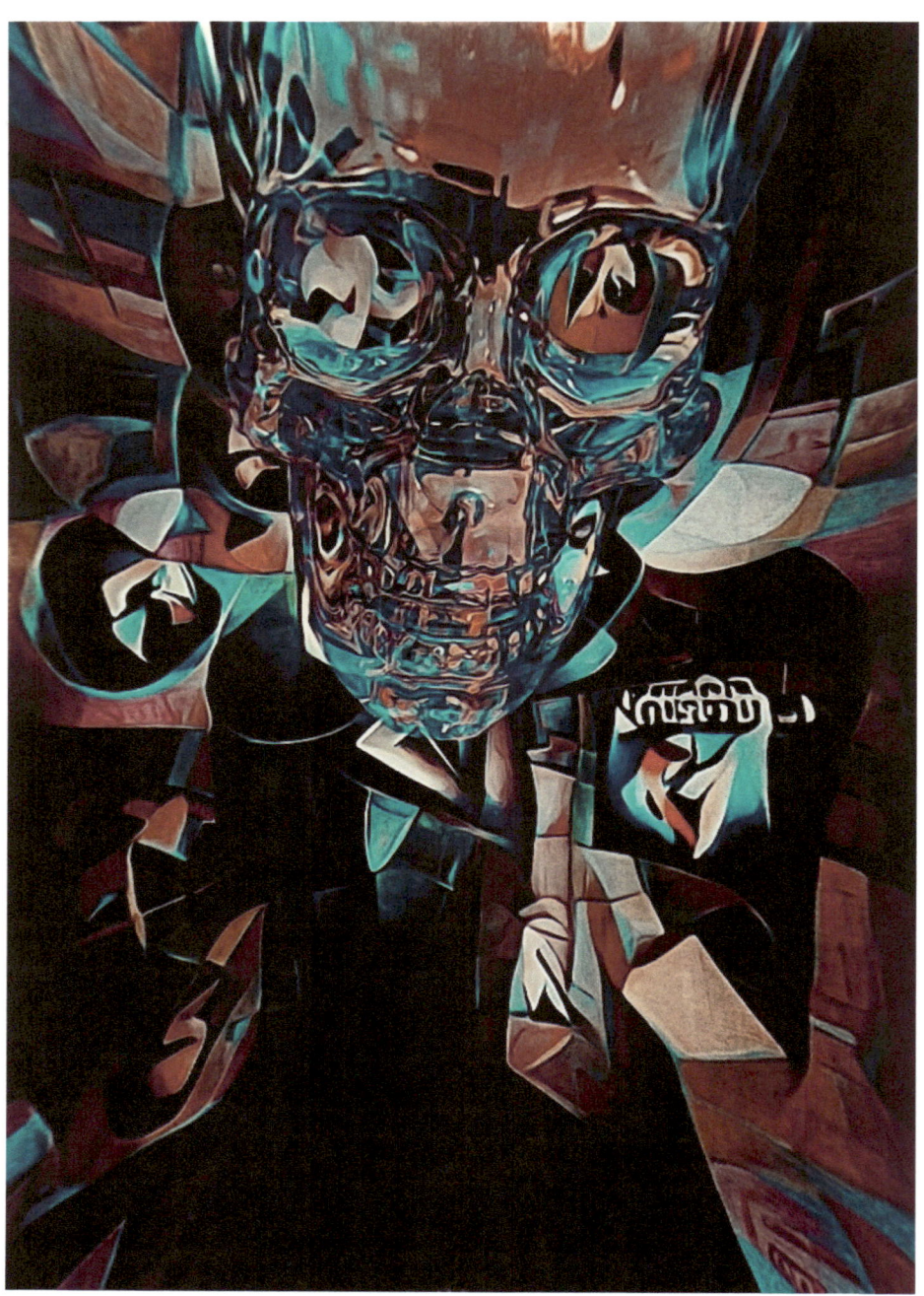

The hollowness inside rings true.

Psalm of the Hyacinth

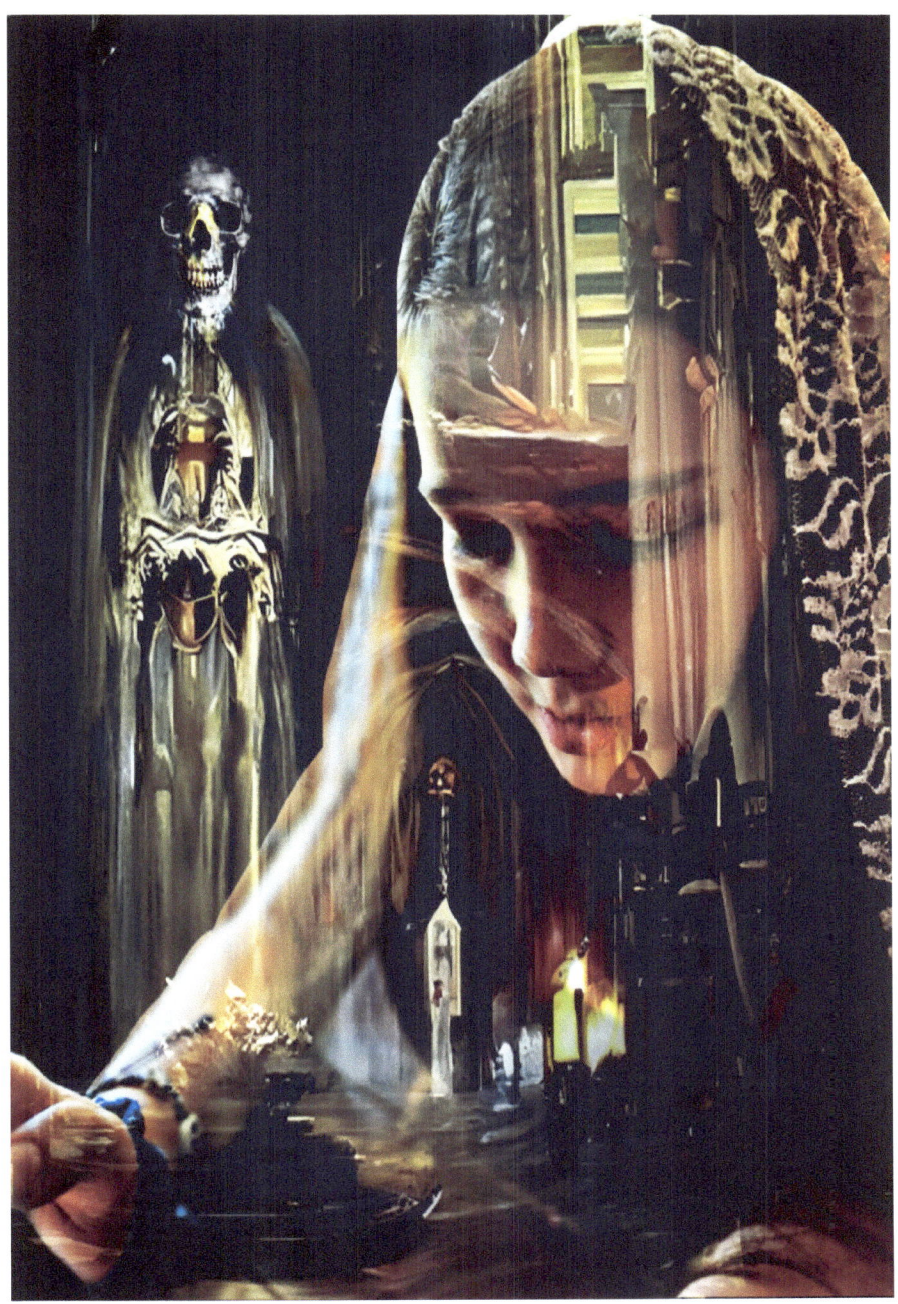

Deep within the cracks of the plinth,

Psalm of the Hyacinth

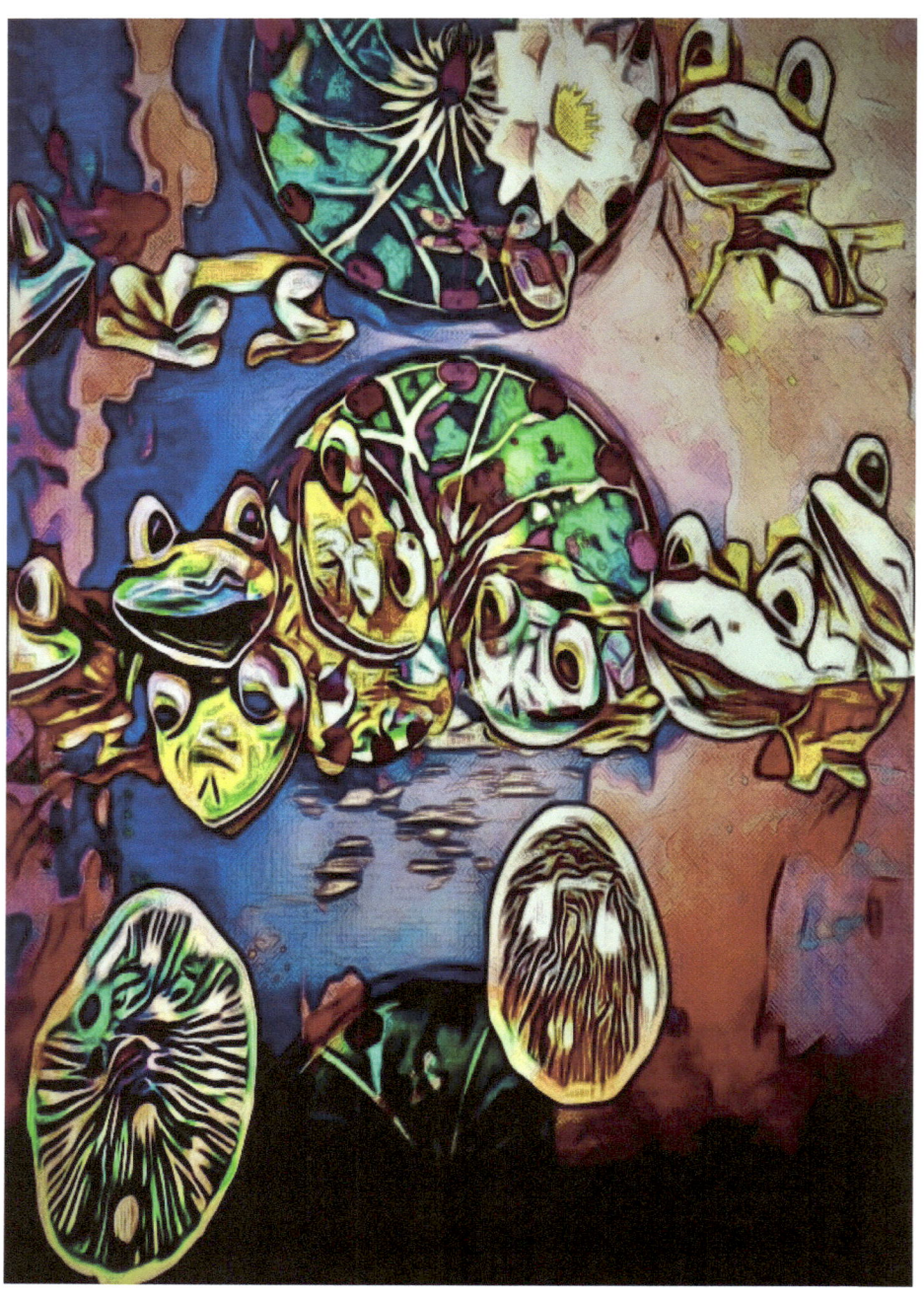

Spring the renewal,

Psalm of the Hyacinth

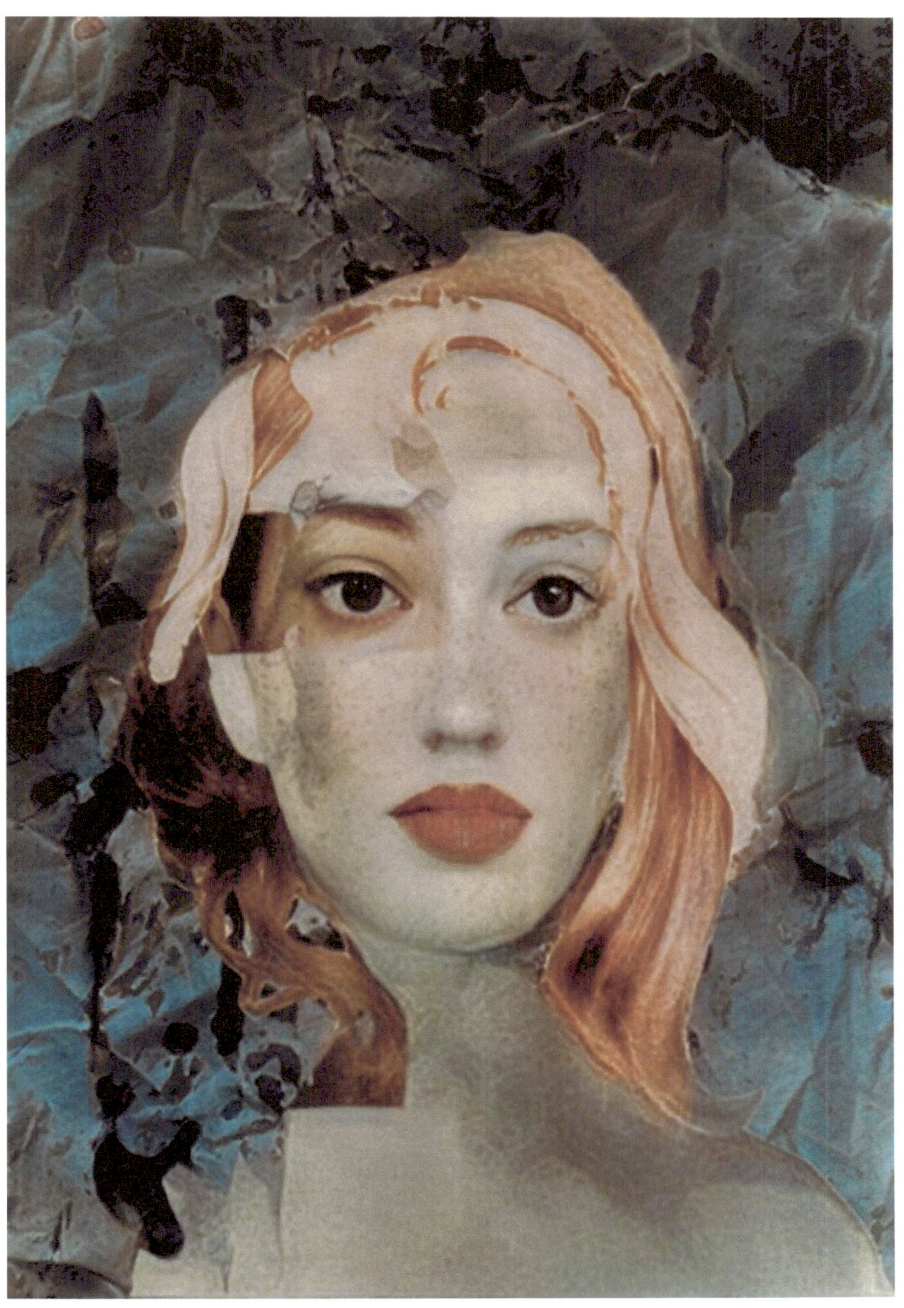

Hyacinth.

Psalm of the Hyacinth

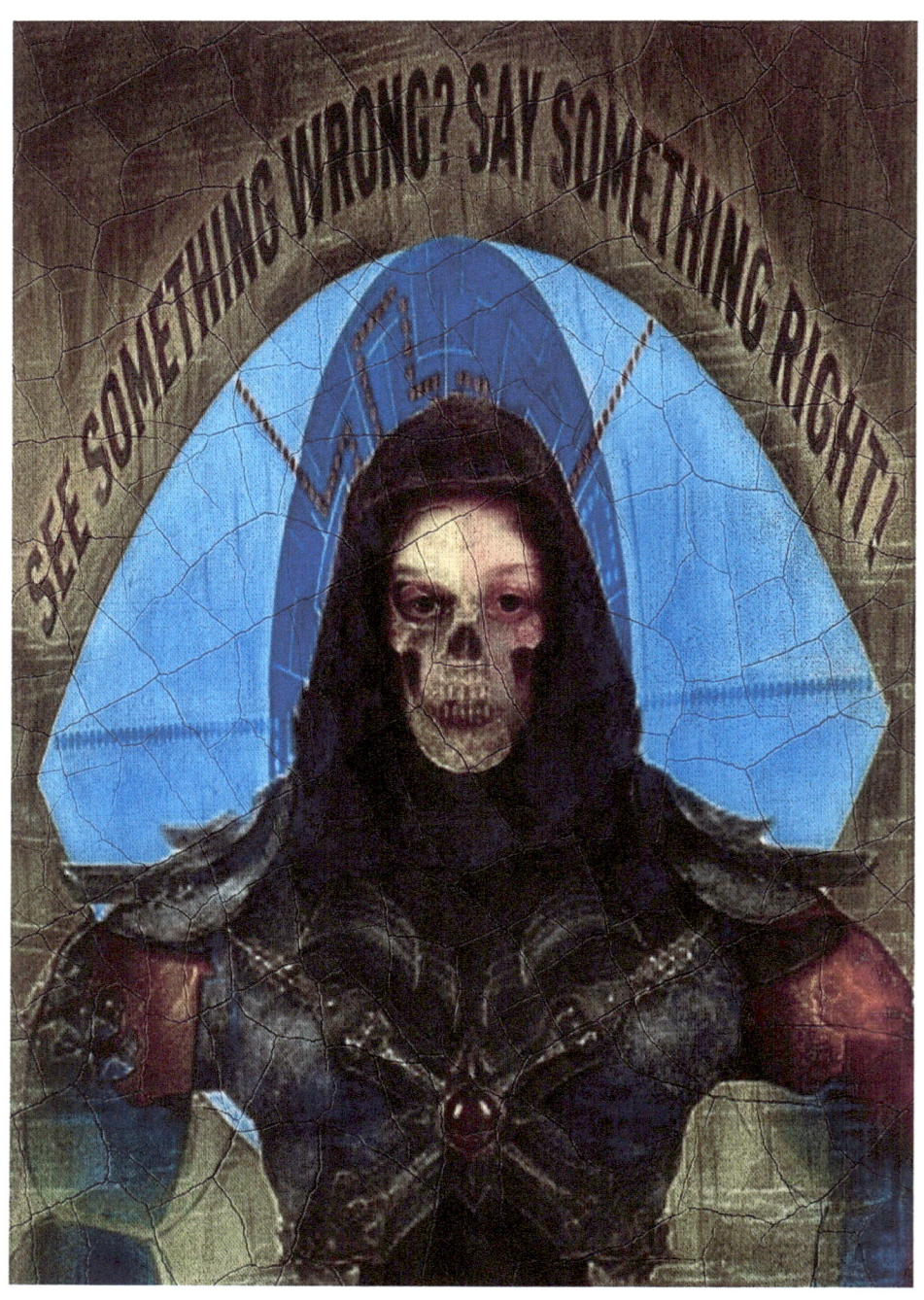

A careless footstep,

Psalm of the Hyacinth

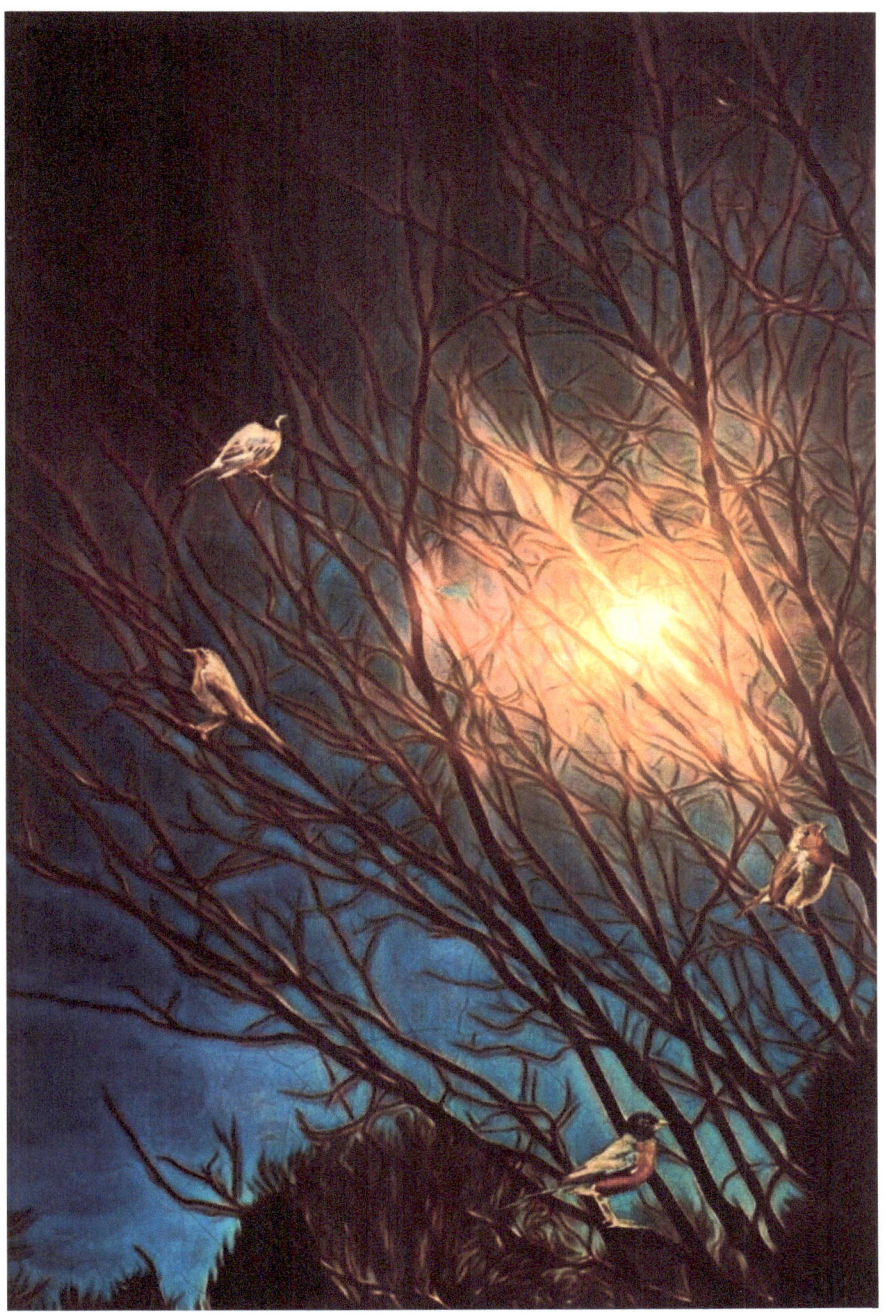

A harsh sun,

Psalm of the Hyacinth

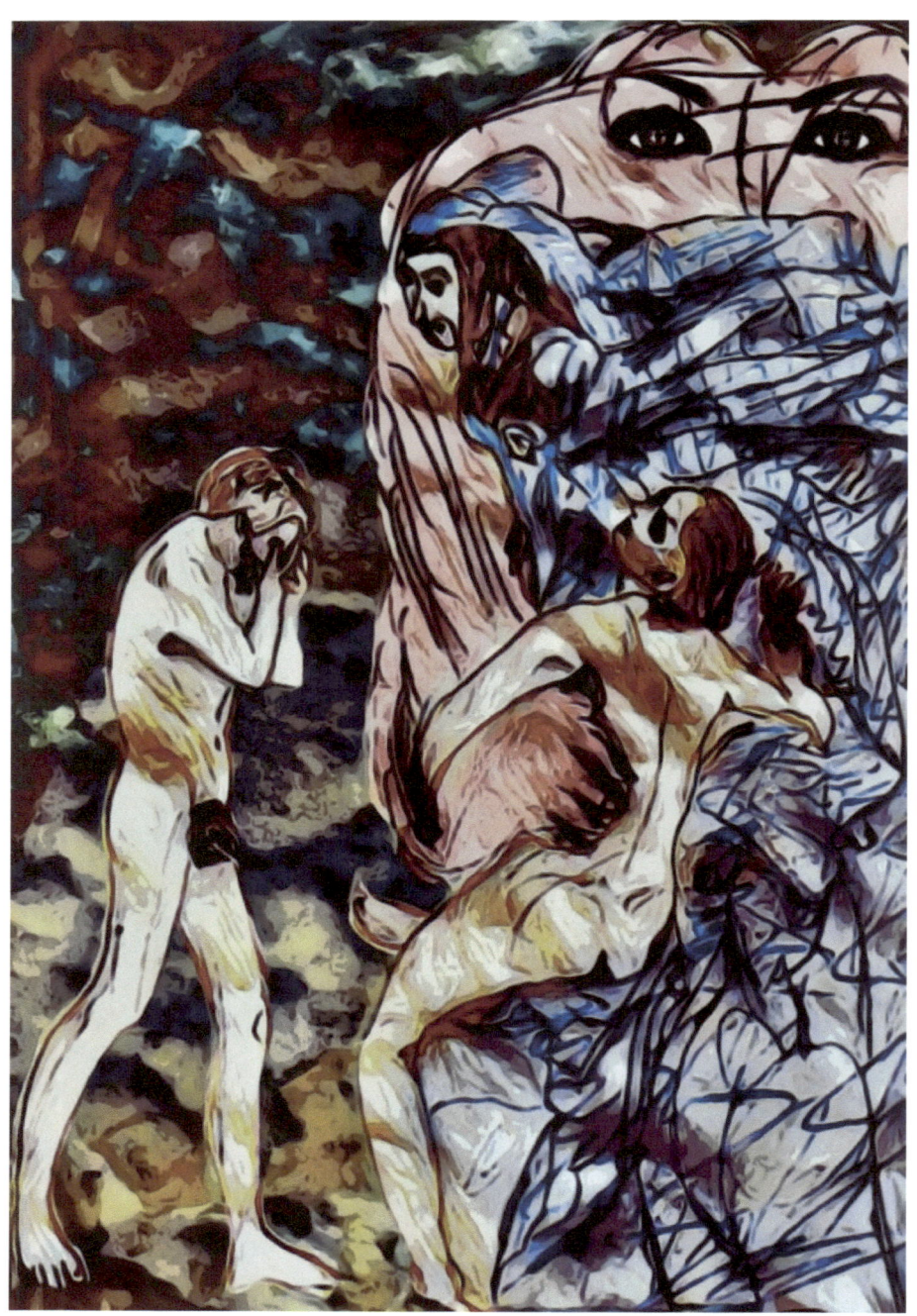

A lover's pluck,

Psalm of the Hyacinth

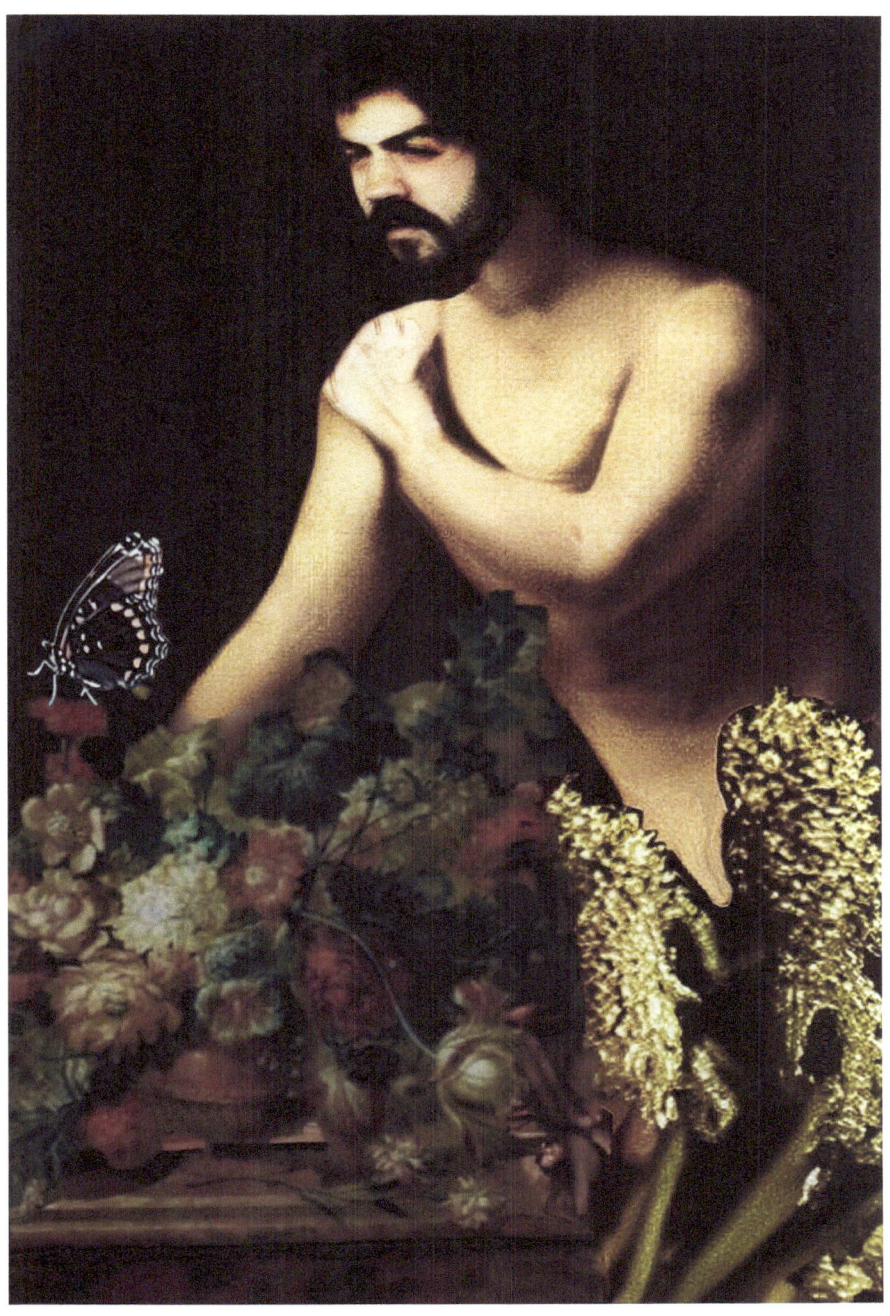

A vase-cutie,

Psalm of the Hyacinth

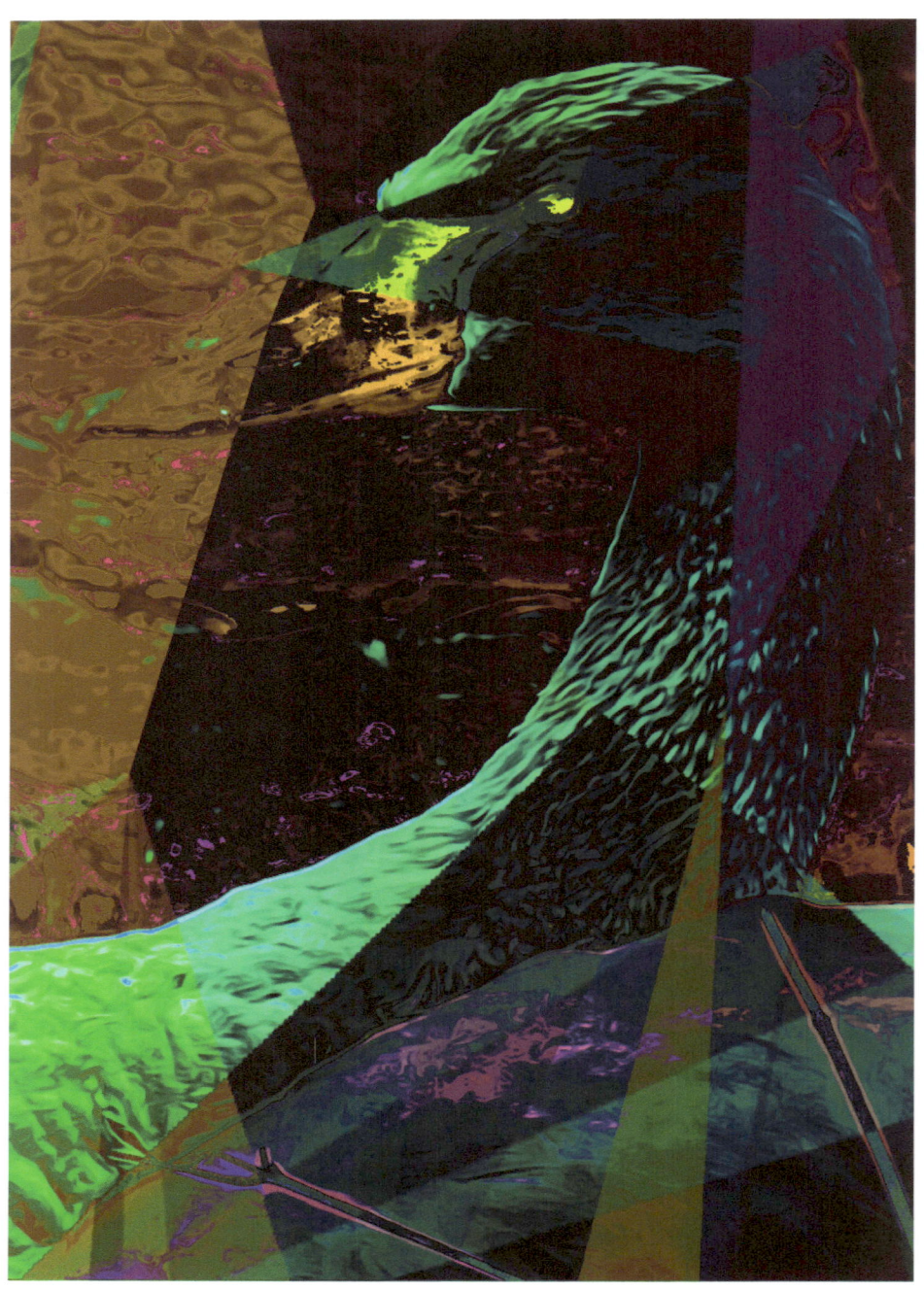

Murder of crows all murders one:

Psalm of the Hyacinth

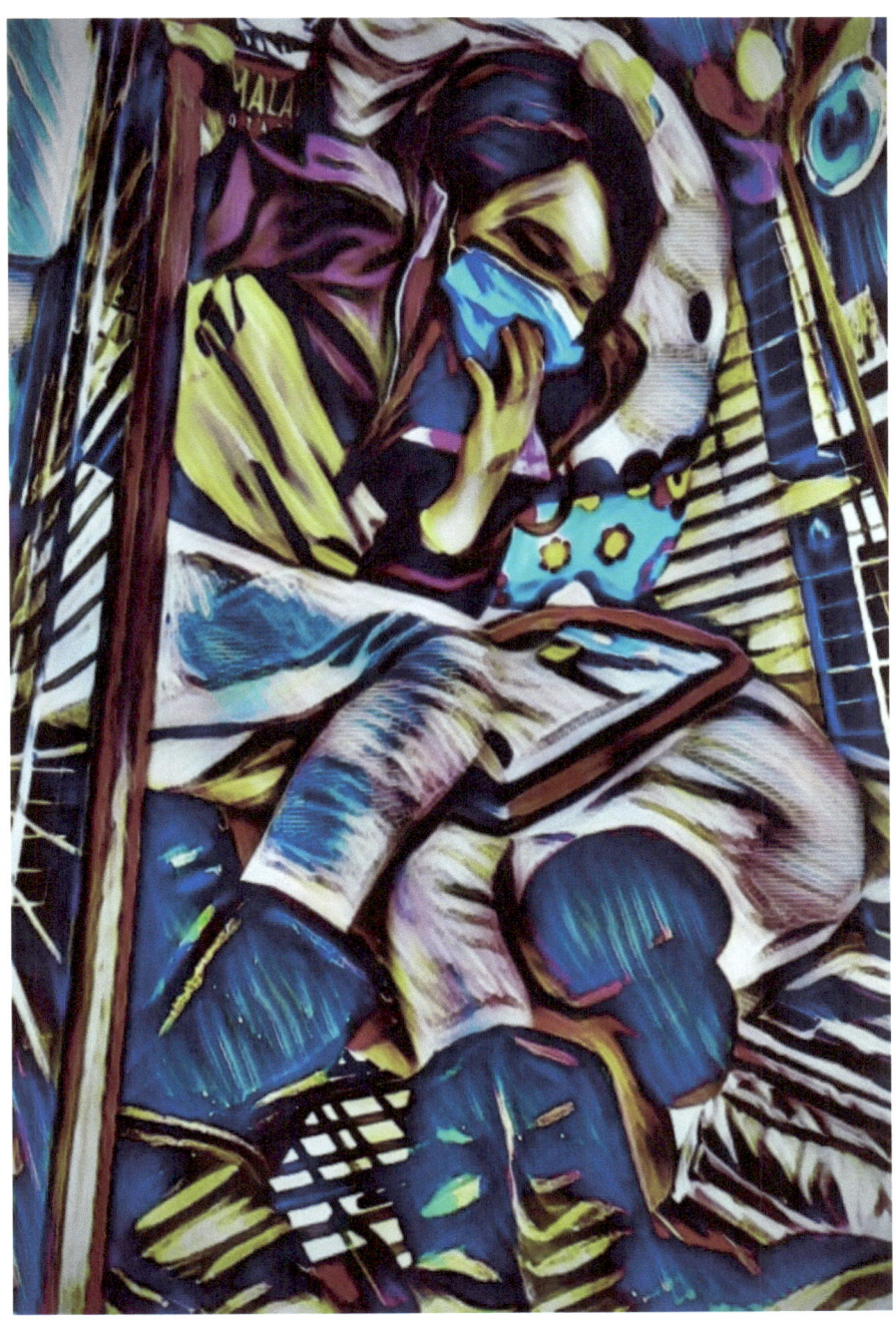

The bloom of hope,

Psalm of the Hyacinth

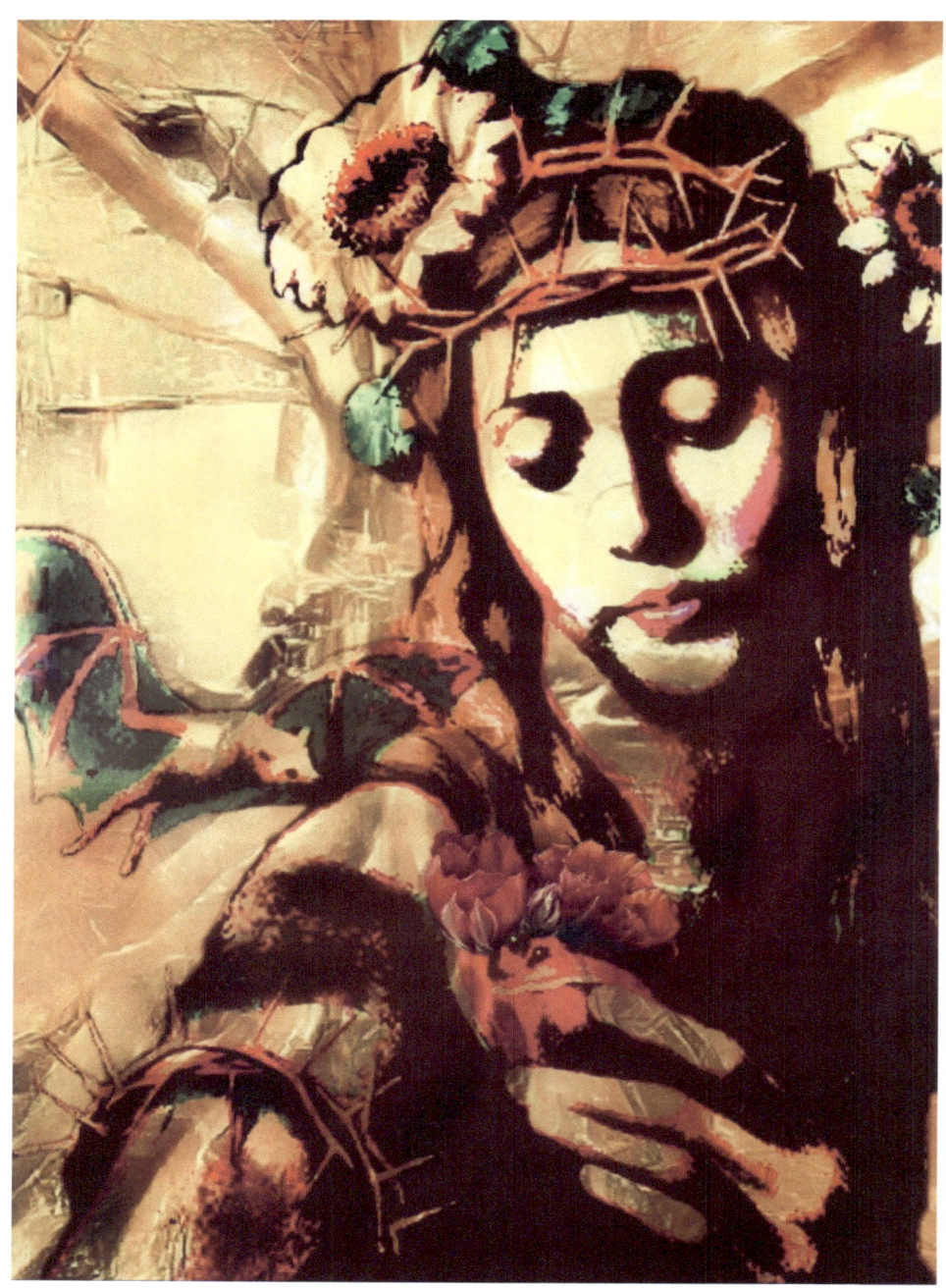

Fragile beauty.

Psalm of the Hyacinth

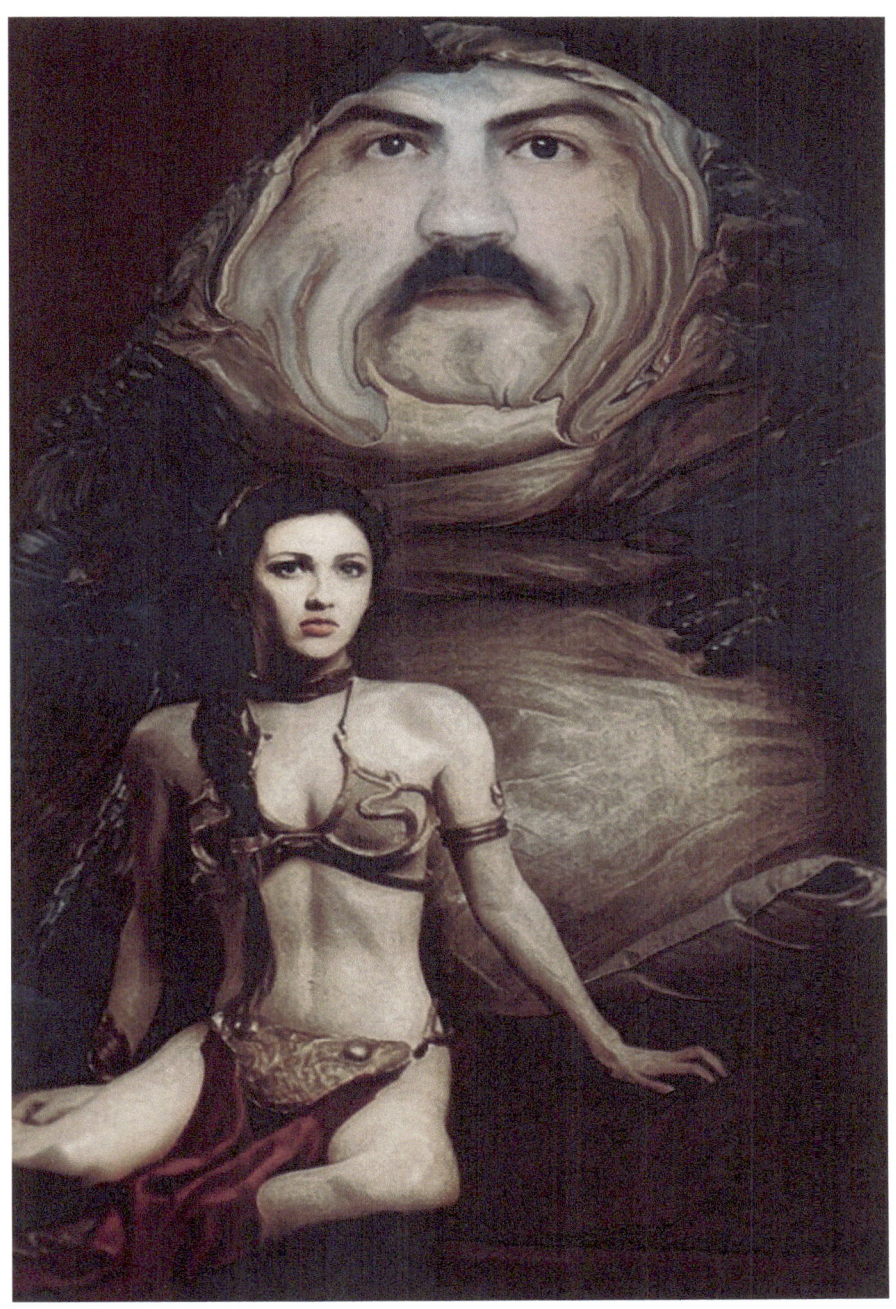

To survive,

Psalm of the Hyacinth

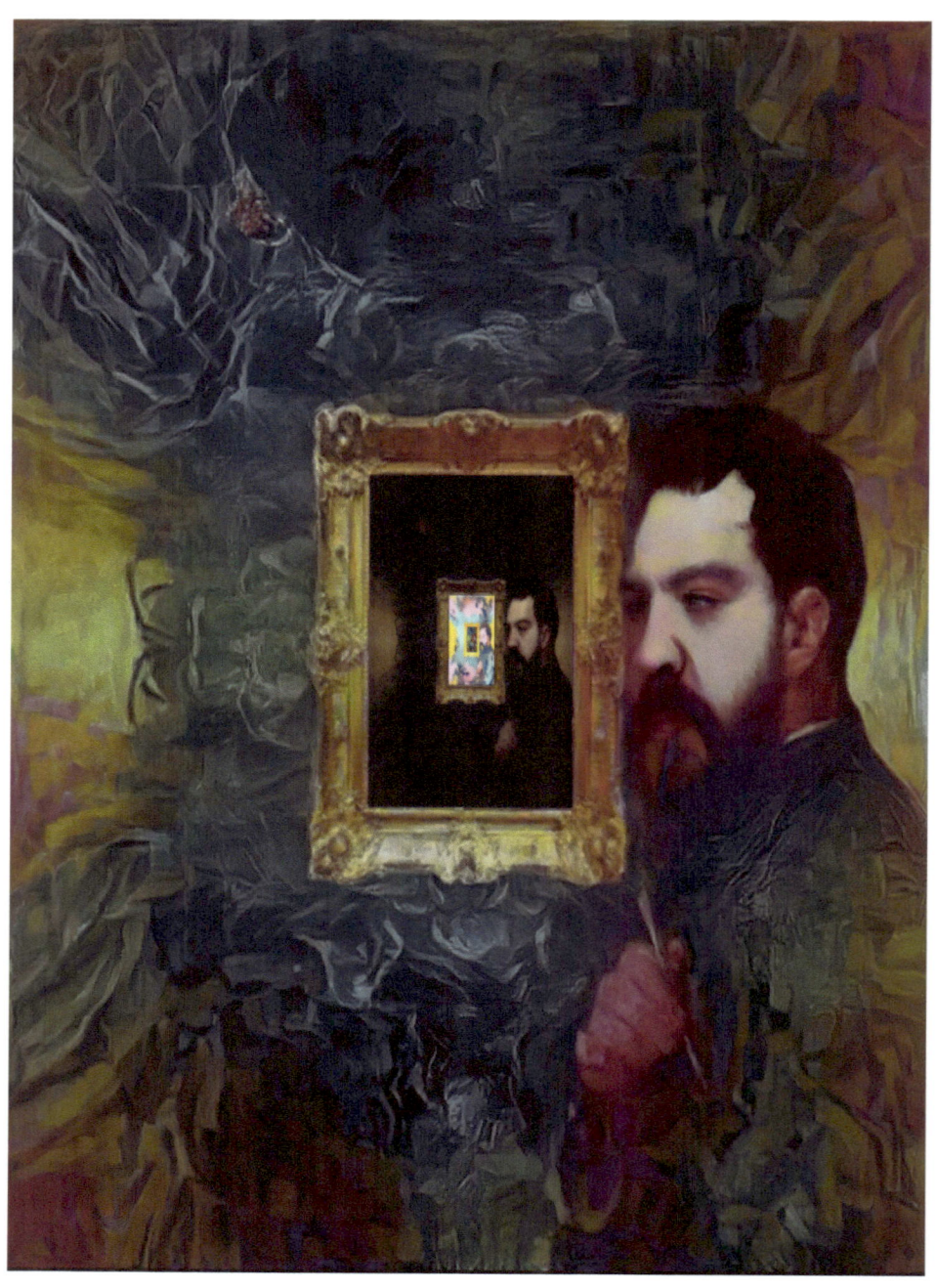

You must borrow down,

Psalm of the Hyacinth

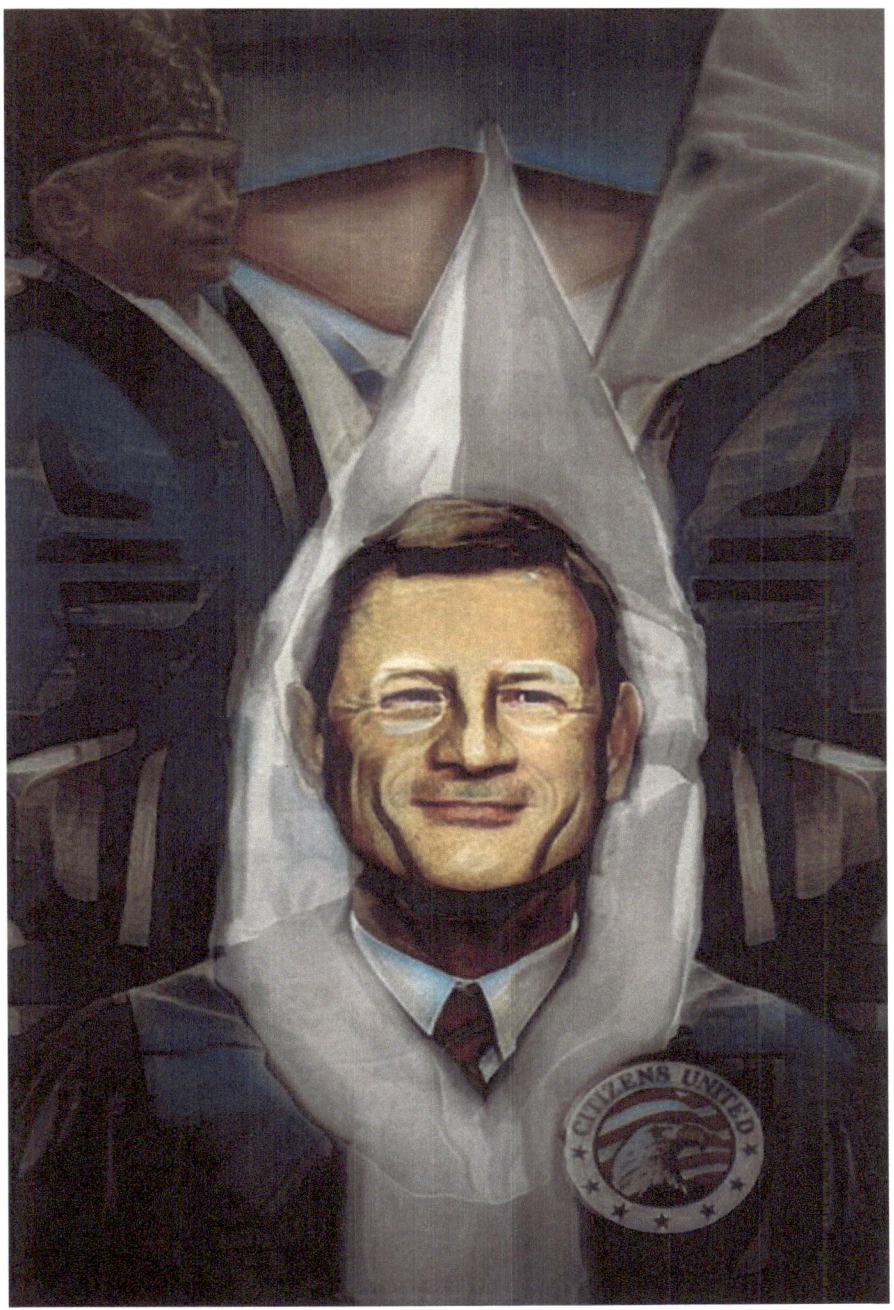

Fight the dirt that can suffocate

Psalm of the Hyacinth

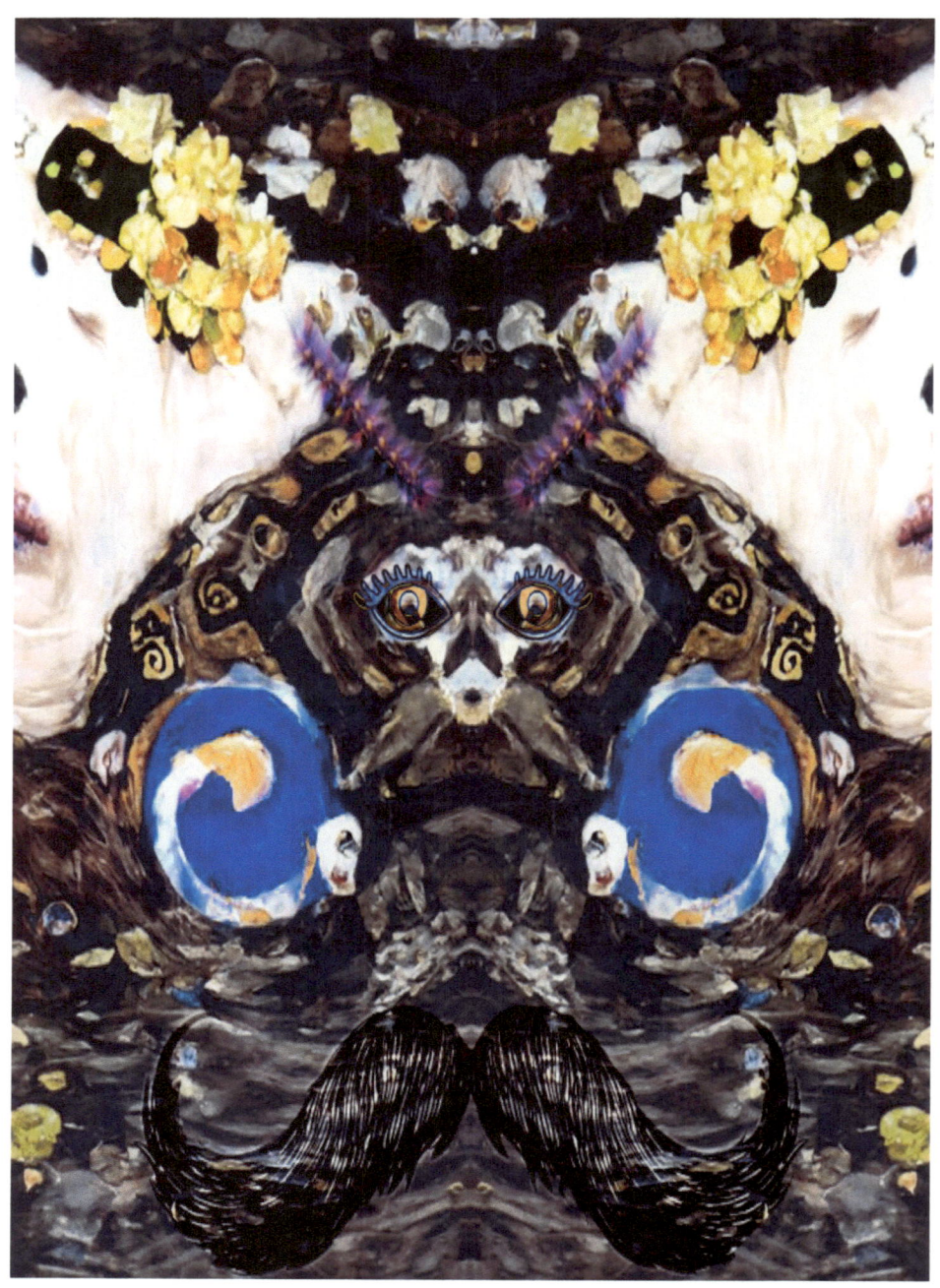

And sprout from a seed,

Psalm of the Hyacinth

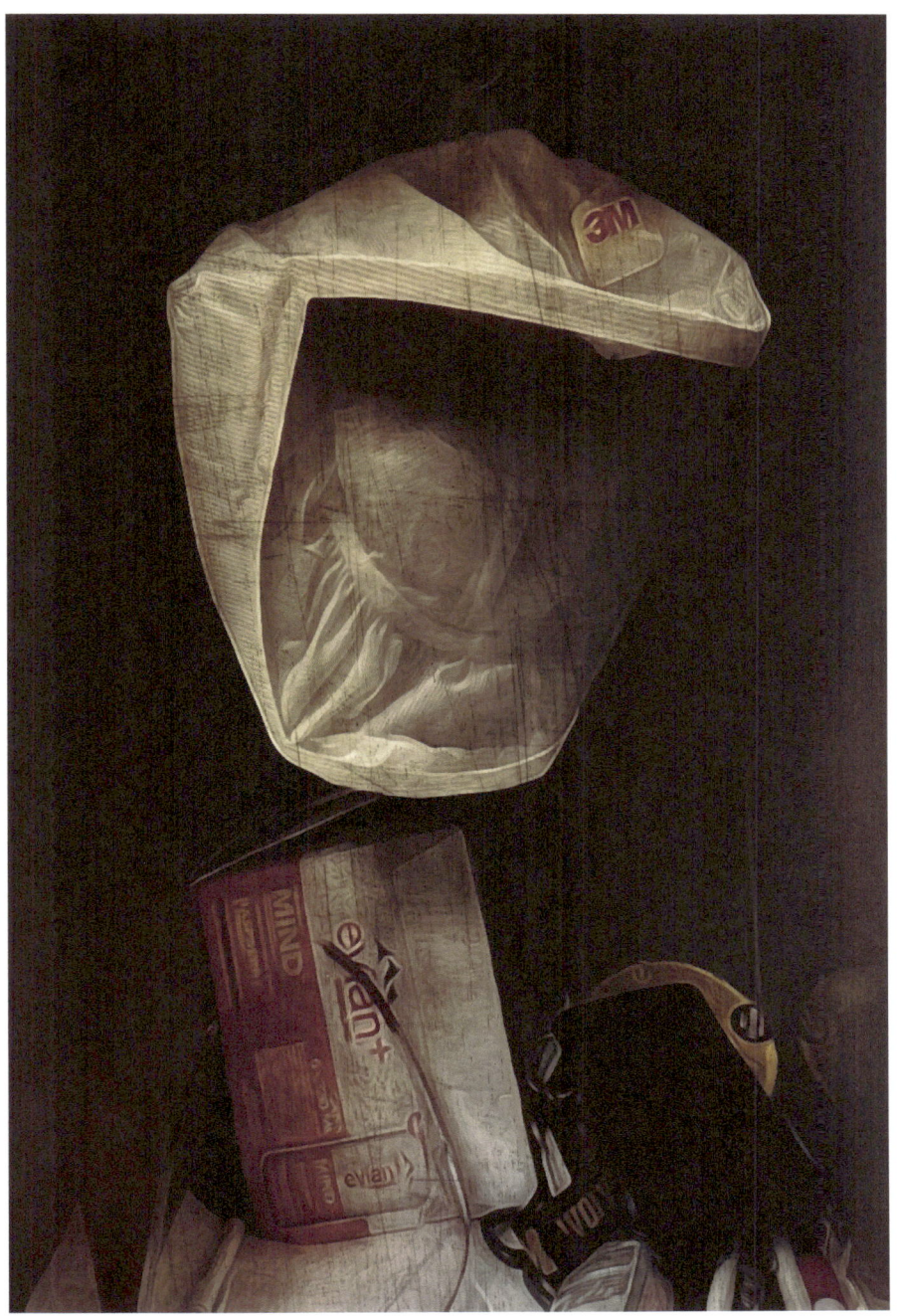

Then the ground-

Psalm of the Hyacinth

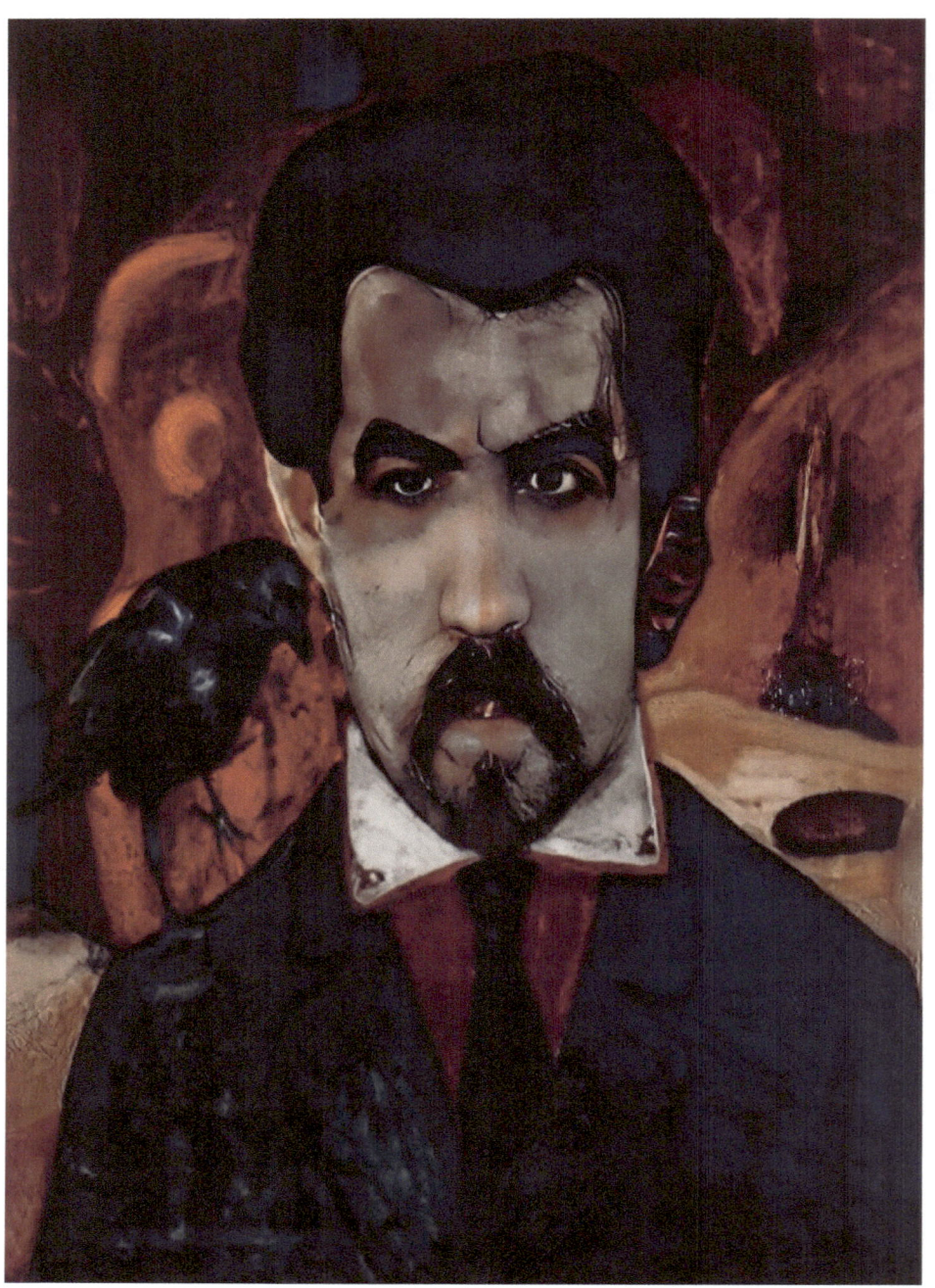

Liberty!

Psalm of the Hyacinth

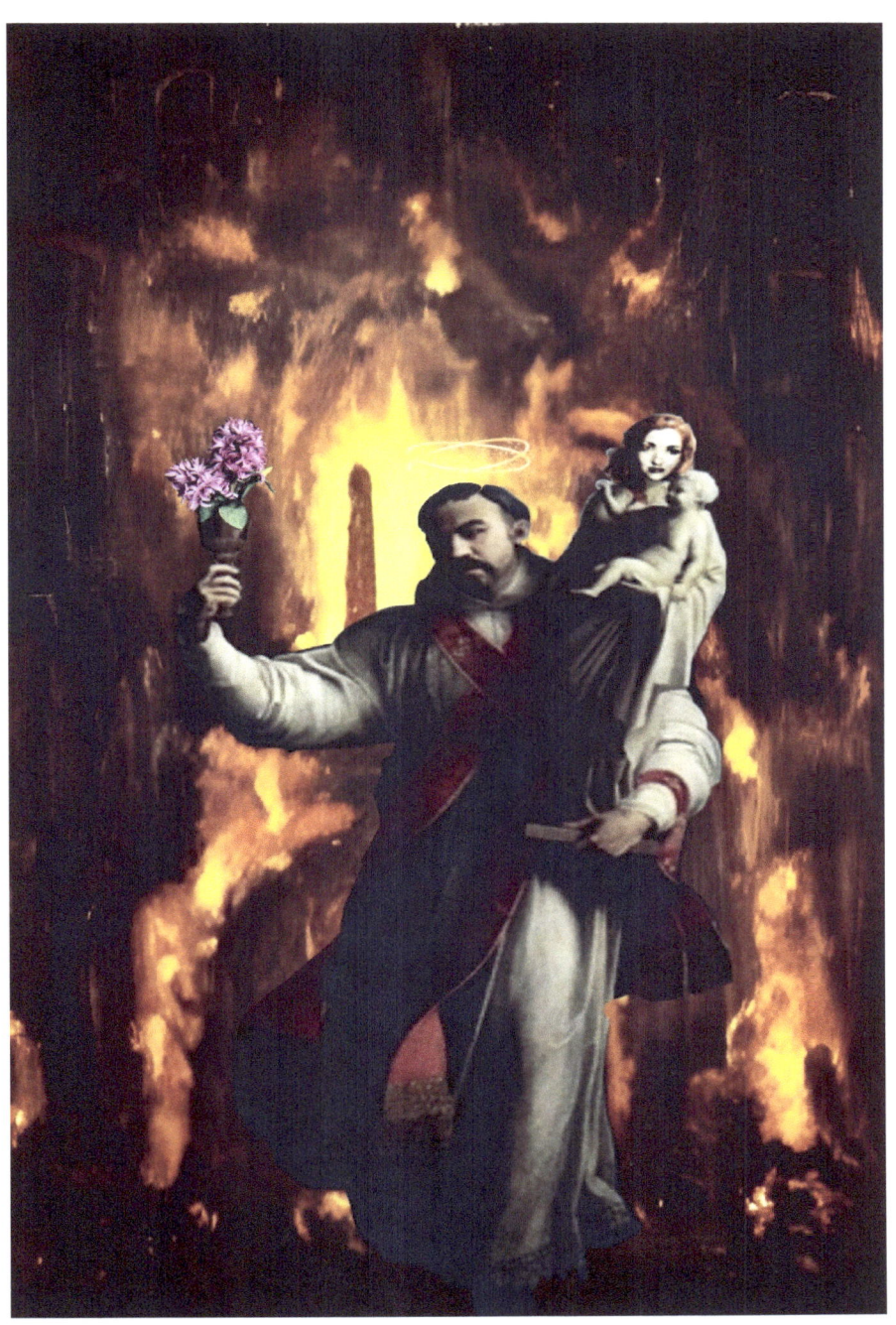

Like a famous saint.

Psalm of the Hyacinth

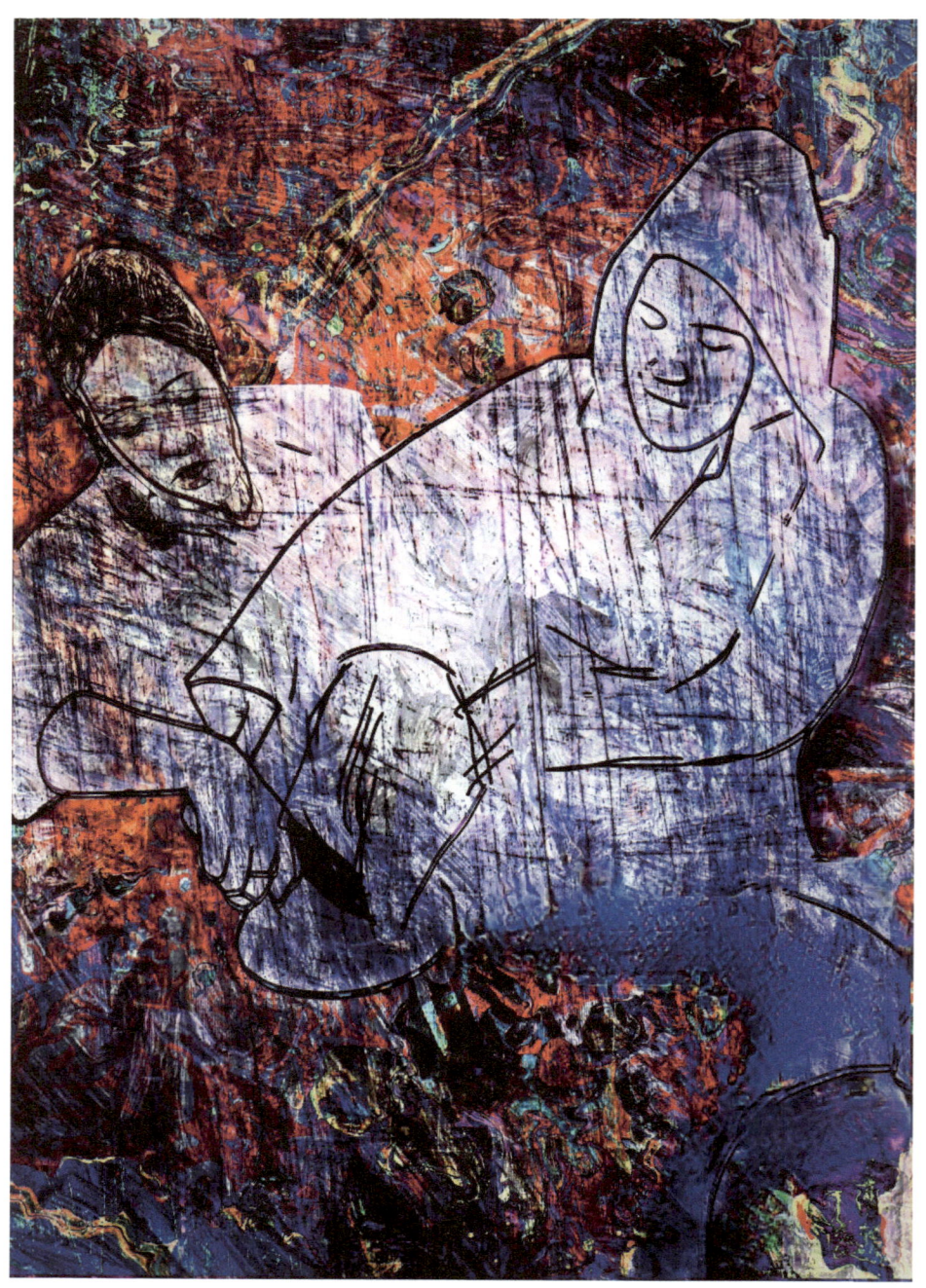

Grow-

Psalm of the Hyacinth

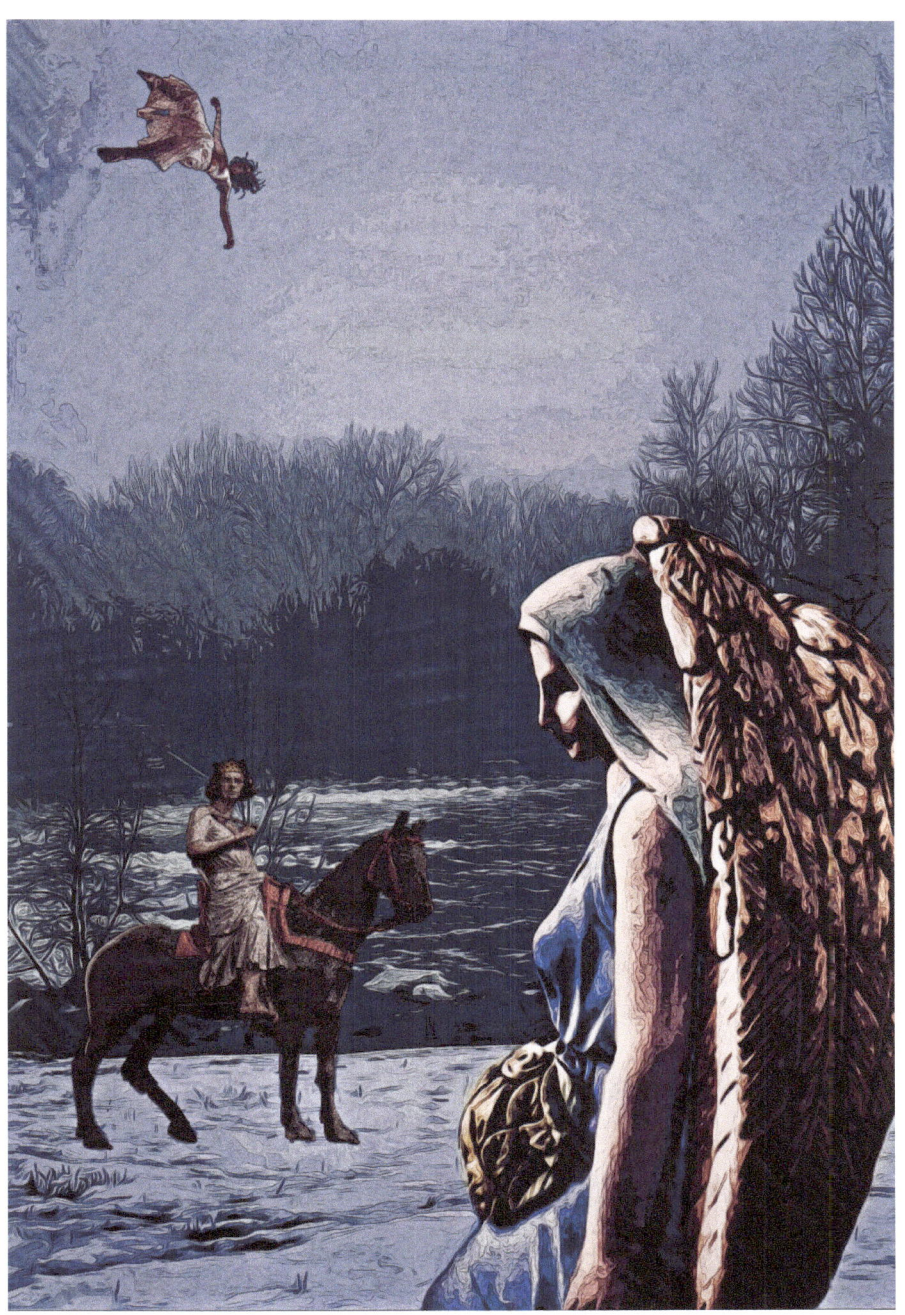

Know the dangers,

Psalm of the Hyacinth

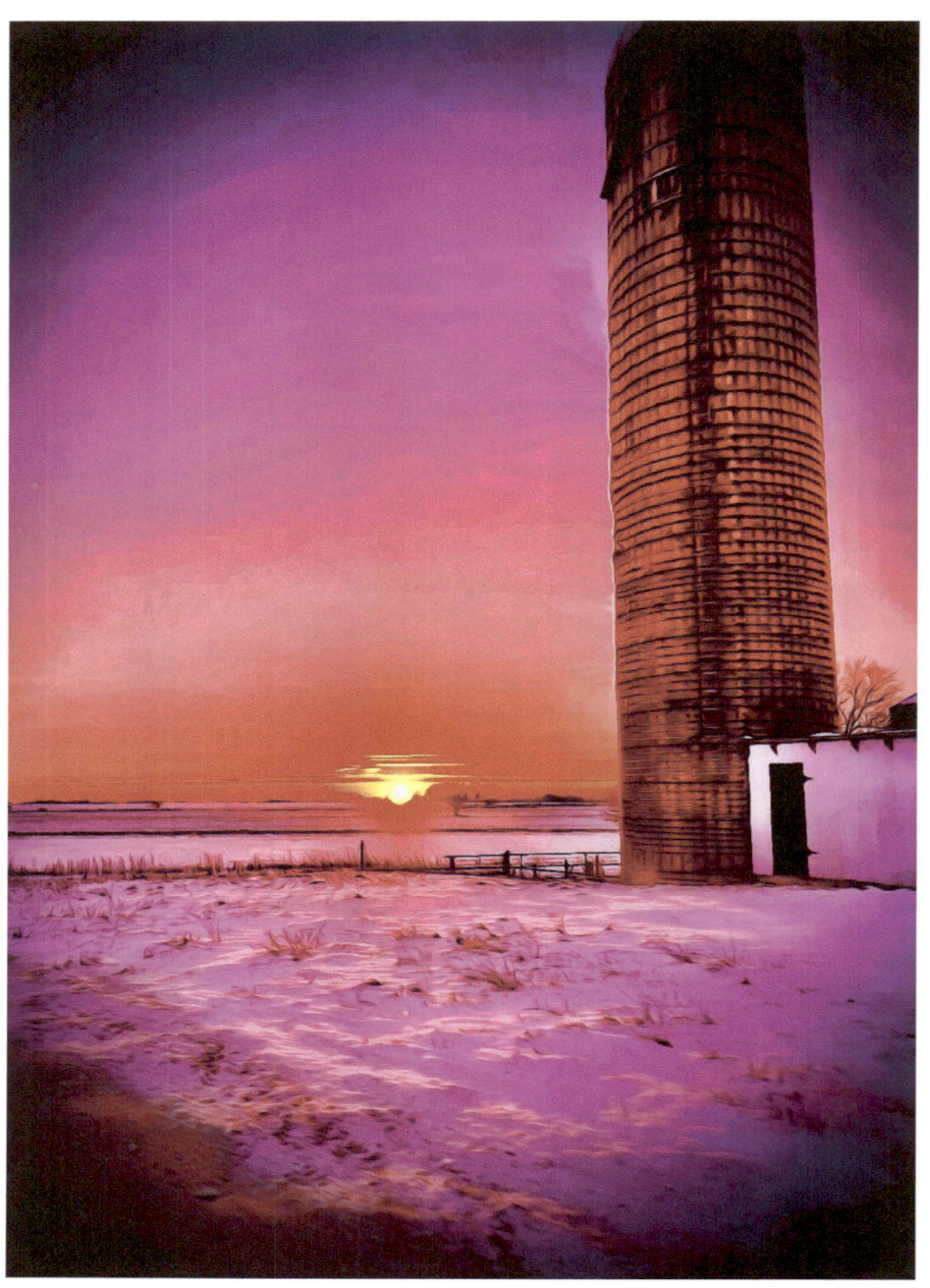

The seasons,

Psalm of the Hyacinth

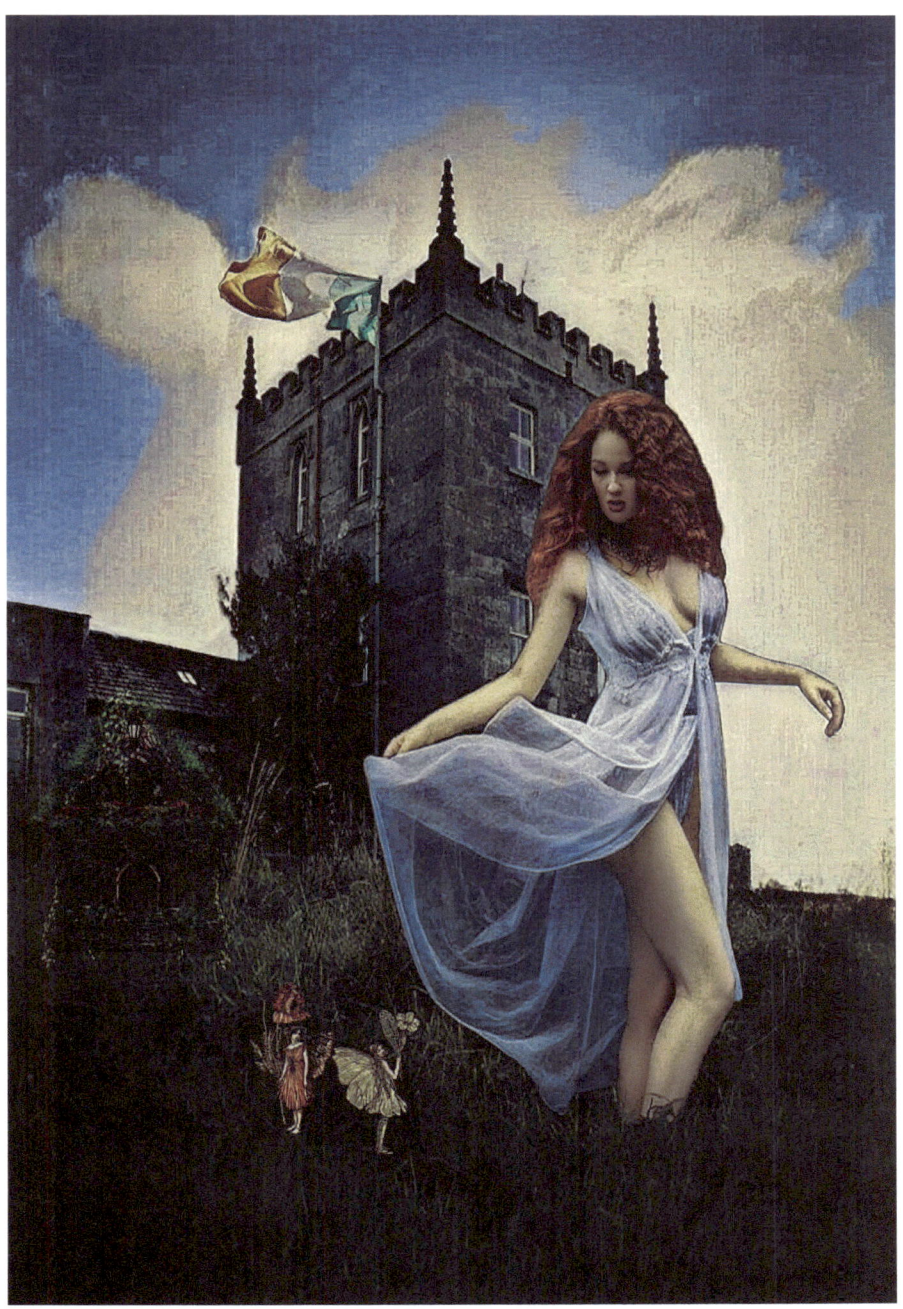

The jealous trample of foot. . .

Psalm of the Hyacinth

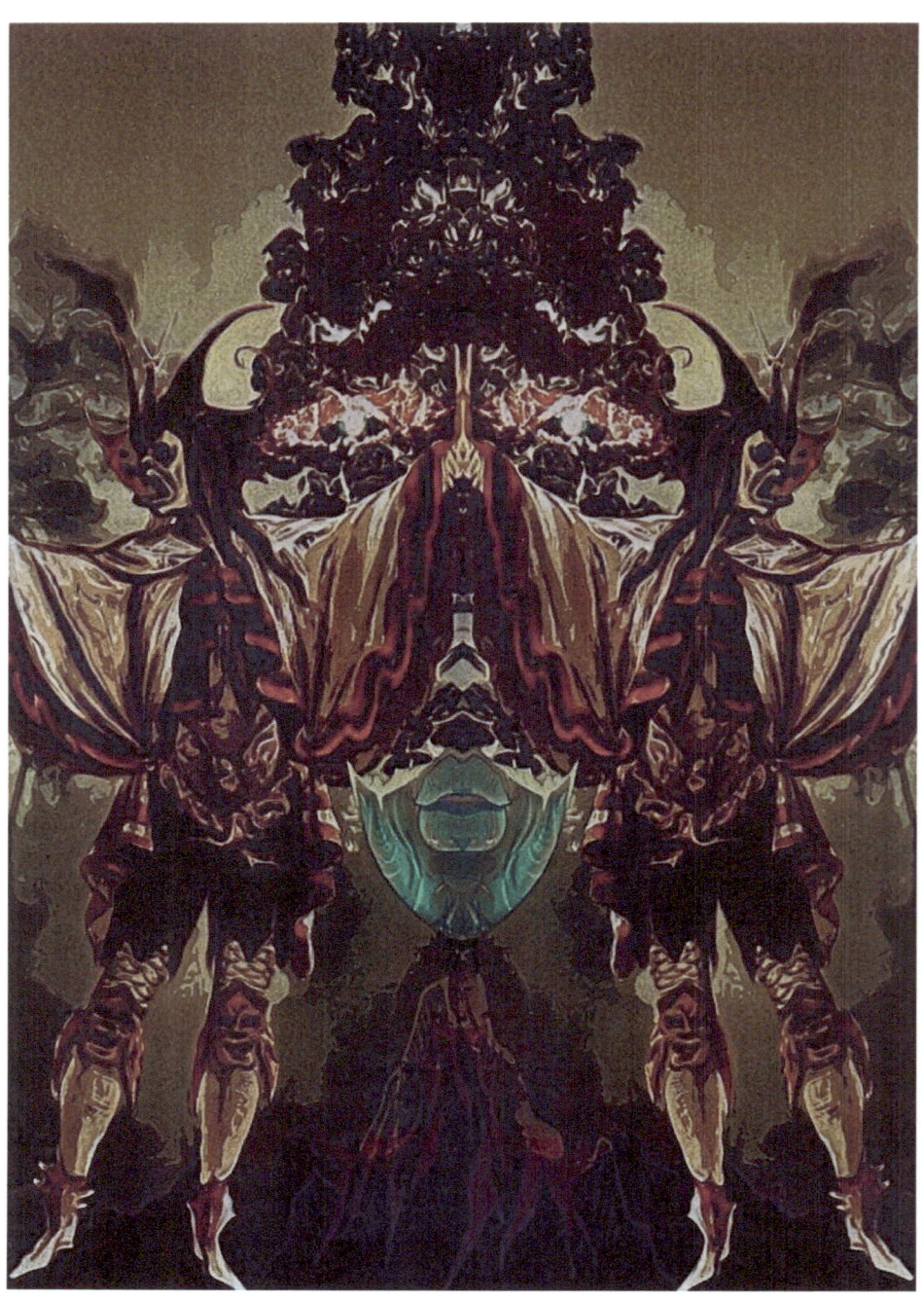

To them you are life in treason.

Psalm of the Hyacinth

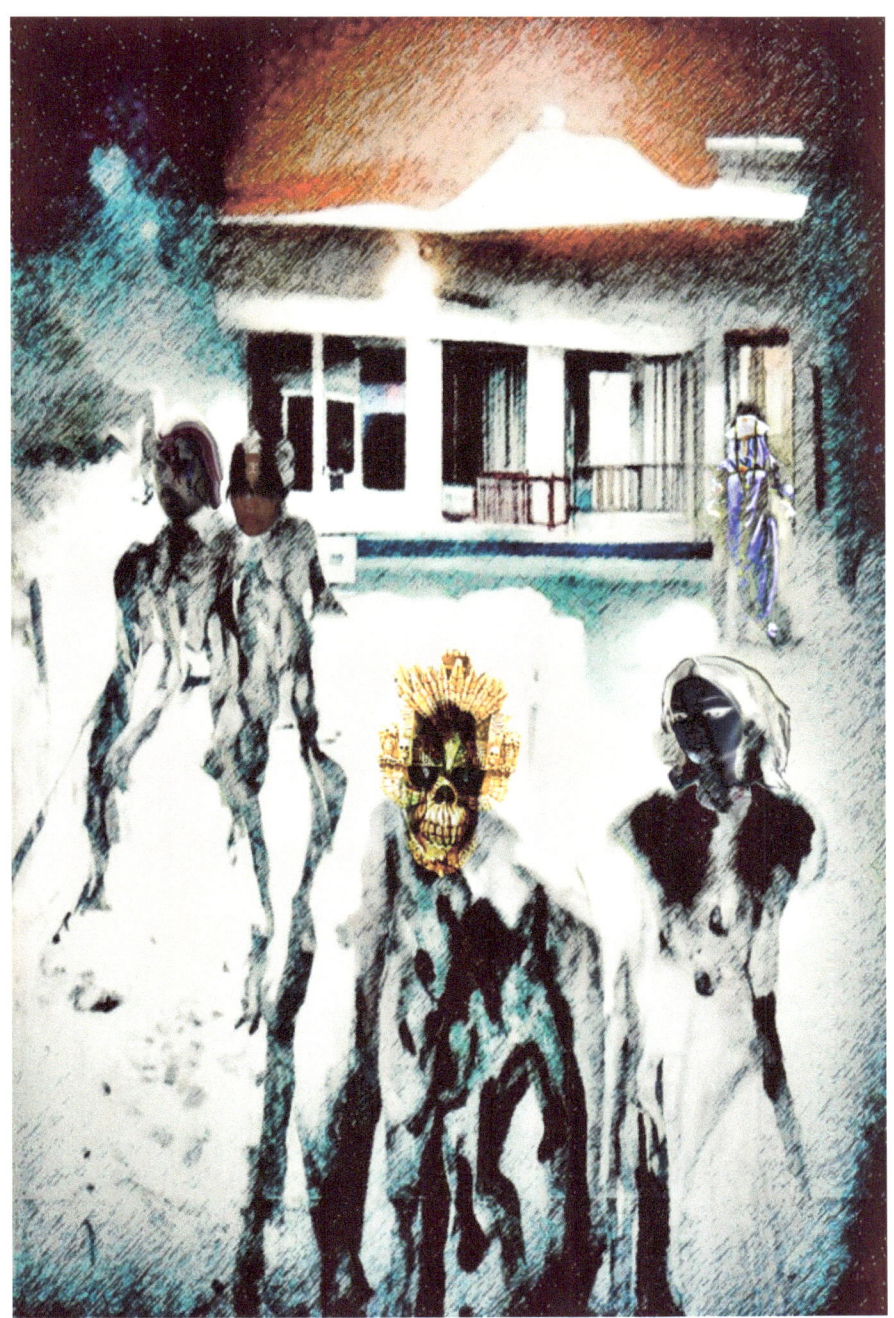

You: smut-diamond among the soot.

Psalm of the Hyacinth

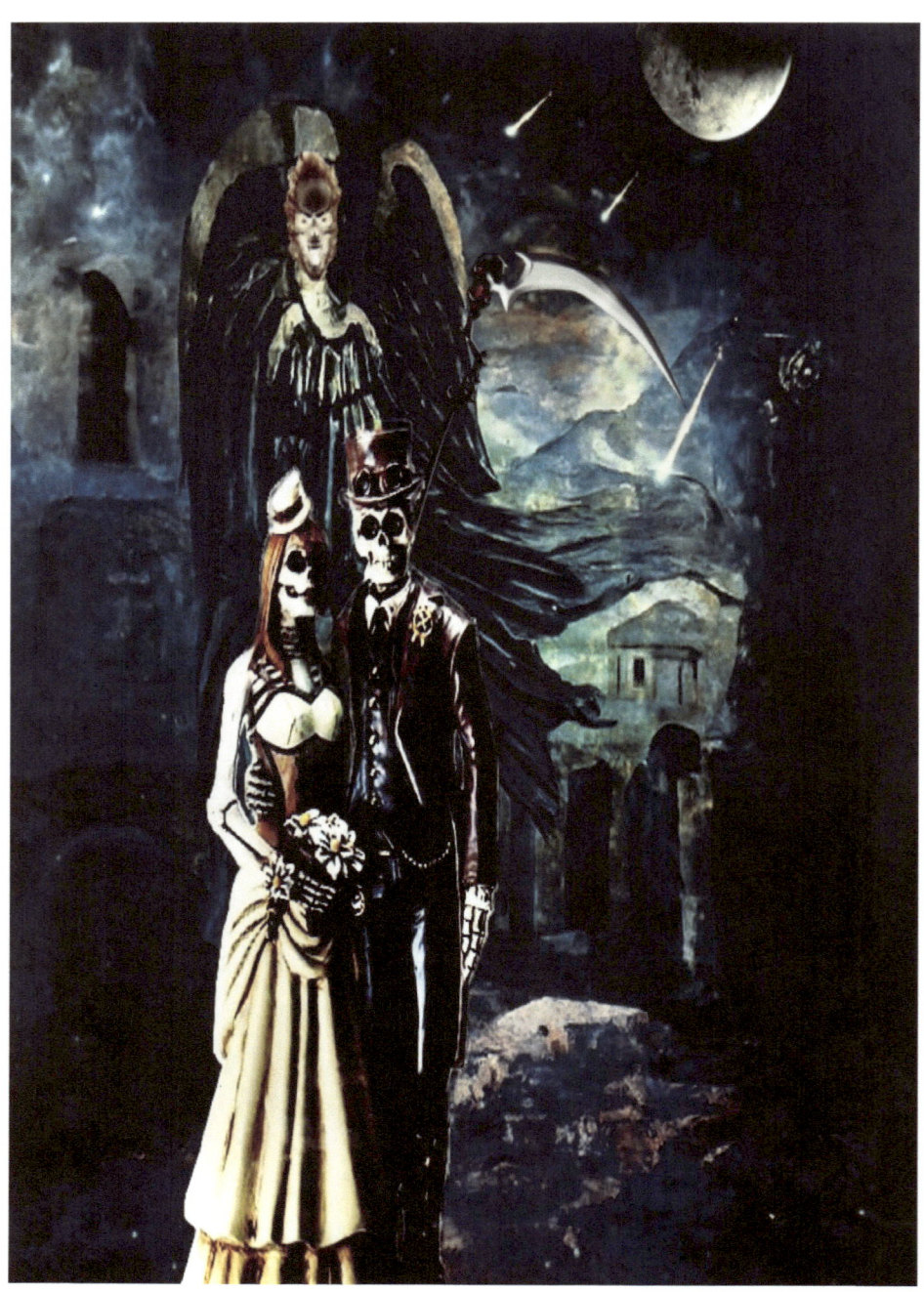

Who else could you share stars-map with?

Psalm of the Hyacinth

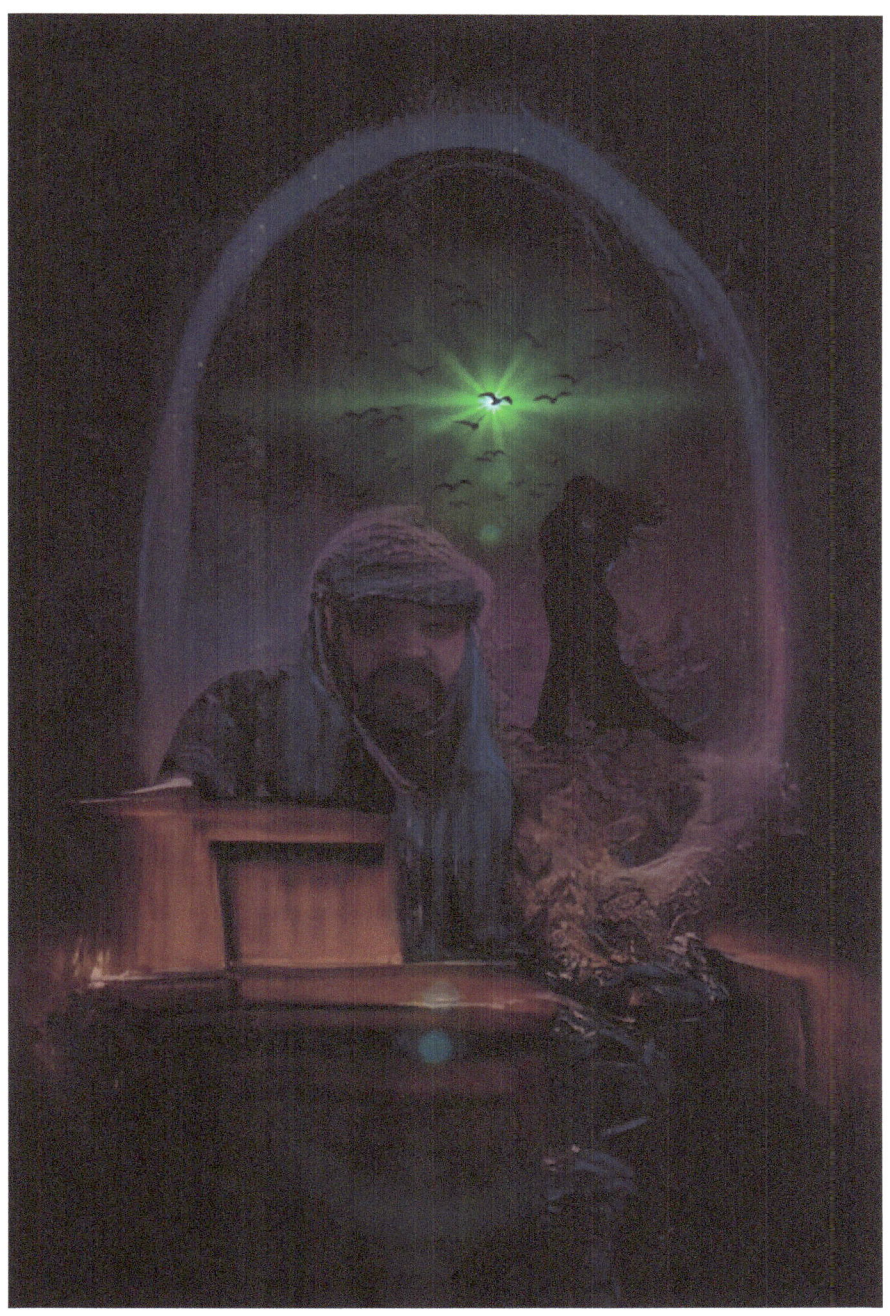

No one but me,

Psalm of the Hyacinth

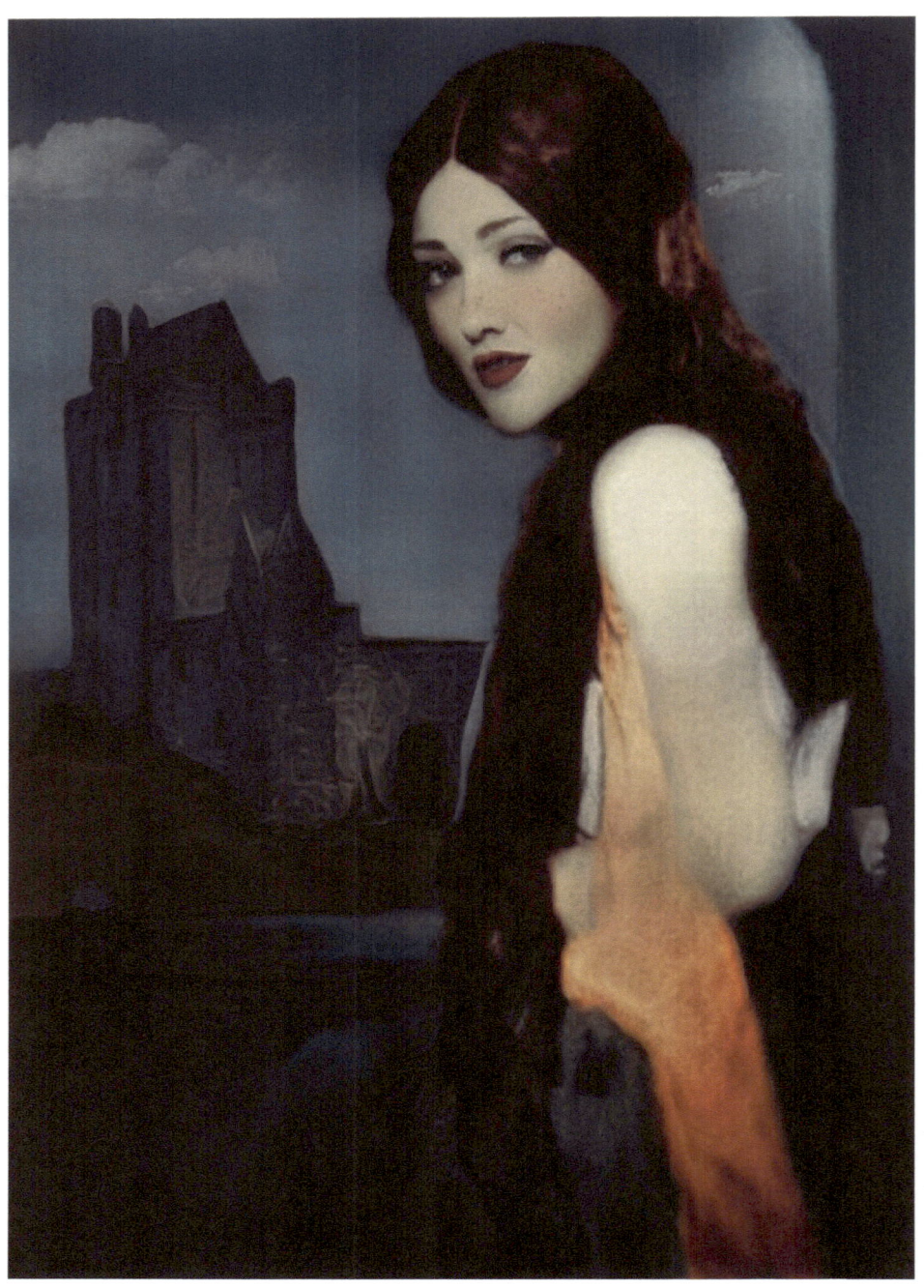

My hyacinth.

Psalm of the Hyacinth

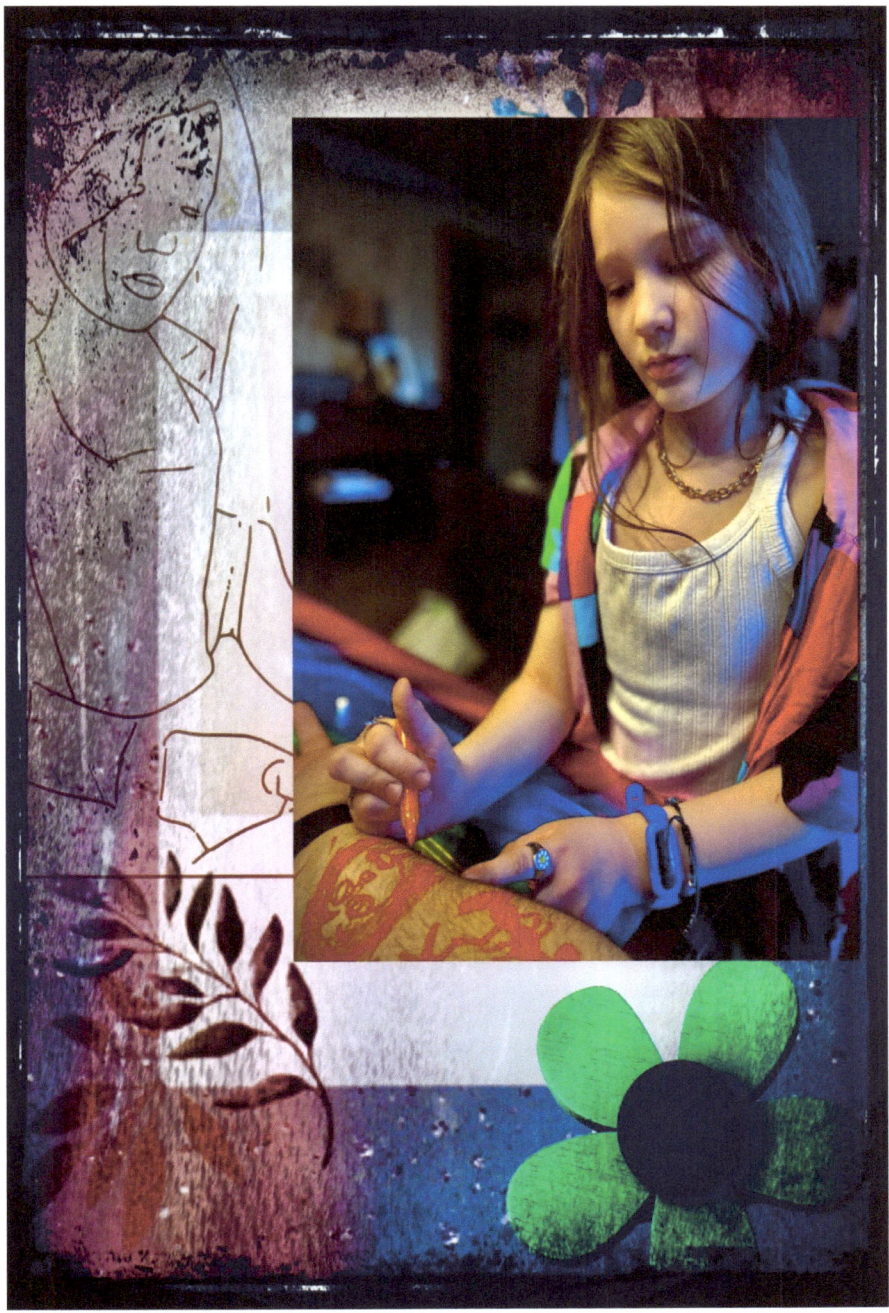

Psalm of the Hyacinth

Torn apart and barely breathing.
Left on the shore. Silence plenty.
All I wanted: notes of singing,
My song on the lips of many
And you to witness the passion;
The madness heard in a chorus.
Long after the flesh has ashen,
Long lives a memory for us-
The trauma of harsh chords in pitch,
The off-rhythm pulse of our thoughts.
Voodoo doll in need of a stitch:
Fate's pin and needles can't be bought.
I left my threads in the labyrinth;
Please follow them, my hyacinth.

Psalm of the Hyacinth

Like Euripides in a cave,
Composing goat odes of torture,
Or De Vere lost in masquerade,
Spear-shaking the loss of nature,
I perform my part for the stage.
You say the lines, full of rhythm,
Storm through the stress, secret in sage.
Be an Oracle but rid phlegm,
The settled state of apathy,
And foretell futures with taboo.
Here cast in bronze, patina green,
The hollowness inside rings true.
Deep within the cracks of the plinth,
Spring the renewal, hyacinth.

Psalm of the Hyacinth

A careless footstep, a harsh sun,
A lover's pluck, a vase-cutie,
Murder of crows all murders one:
The bloom of hope, fragile beauty.
To survive, you must borrow down,
Fight the dirt that can suffocate
And sprout from a seed, then the ground-
Liberty! like a famous saint.
Grow- know the dangers, the seasons,
The jealous trample of foot. . .
To them you are life in treason.
You: smut-diamond among the soot.
Who else could you share stars-map with?
No one but me, my hyacinth.

www.ingramcontent.com/pod-product-compliance
Lightning Source LLC
Chambersburg PA
CBHW040322220526
45473CB00009B/2538